P9-APQ-245

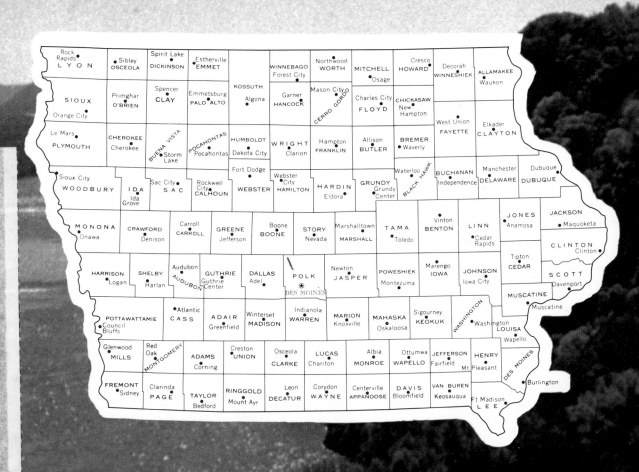

The New
Enchantment of America
IOWA

By Allan Carpenter

CHILDRENS PRESS, CHICAGO

ACKNOWLEDGMENTS

For assistance in the preparation of the revised edition, the author thanks:
THE IOWA DEVELOPMENT COMMISSION, Des Moines.

American Airlines—Anne Vitaliano, Director of Public Relations; *Capitol Historical Society,* Washington, D. C.; *Newberry Library,* Chicago, Dr. Lawrence Towner, Director; *Northwestern University Library,* Evanston, Illinois; *United Airlines*—John P. Grember, Manager of Special Promotions; Joseph P. Hopkins, Manager, News Bureau; Carl Provorse, *Carpenter Publishing House.*

UNITED STATES GOVERNMENT AGENCIES: *Department of Agriculture*—Robert Hailstock, Jr., Photography Division, Office of Communication; Donald C. Schuhart, Information Division, Soil Conservation Service. *Army*—Doran Topolosky, Public Affairs Office, Chief of Engineers, Corps of Engineers. *Department of Interior*—Louis Churchville, Director of Communications; EROS Space Program—Phillis Wiepking, Community Affairs; Charles Withington, Geologist; Mrs. Ruth Herbert, Information Specialist; Bureau of Reclamation; National Park Service—Fred Bell and the individual sites; Fish and Wildlife Service—Bob Hines, Public Affairs Office. *Library of Congress*—Dr. Alan Fern, Director of the Department of Research; Sara Wallace, Director of Publications; Dr. Walter W. Ristow, Chief, Geography and Map Division; Herbert Sandborn, Exhibits Officer. *National Archives*—Dr. James B. Rhoads, Archivist of the United States; Albert Meisel, Assistant Archivist for Educational Programs; David Eggenberger, Publications Director; Bill Leary, Still Picture Reference; James Moore, Audio-Visual Archives. *United States Postal Service*—Herb Harris, Stamps Division.

For assistance in the preparation of the first edition, the author thanks:
William J. Petersen, Superintendent, the State Historical Society of Iowa; David Archie, Editor, *The Iowan* magazine; Iowa State Department of History and Archives; State Printing Board; Marshall R. Beard, Registrar, State College of Iowa.

Illustrations on the preceding pages:
Cover photograph: Iowa farm, USDA, Robert Hailstock
Page 1: Commemorative stamps of historic interest
Pages 2-3: The Great River Road (Mississippi), USDI, NPS, Effigy Mounds National Monument
Page 3: (Map) USDI Geological Survey
Pages 4-5: Des Moines area, EROS Space Photo, USDI Geological Survey, EROS Data Center

Project Editor, Revised Edition:
Joan Downing
Assistant Editor, Revised Edition:
Mary Reidy

Library of Congress Cataloging in Publication Data

Carpenter, John Allan, 1917-
Iowa.

(His The new enchantment of America)
SUMMARY: Discusses the history, geography, resources, and famous citizens of the Hawkeye State. Also spotlights numerous places of interest.
1. Iowa—Juvenile literature.
[1. Iowa] I. Title. II. Series.
F621.3.C3 1979   977.7   79-11802
ISBN 0-516-04115-0

Contents

A True Story to Set the Scene

NEW TASTE FROM IOWA

When an unusually heavy blizzard swept into Iowa in November 1942, it struck down one of the state's most famous "residents."

This story began back in 1881, when Jesse Hiatt was strolling through his orchard near Peru, Iowa, in Madison County. He was pleased to see that his yellow belleflower apple tree had grown new shoots on the top, and the shoots were blossoming. Because the top of the tree had been destroyed by bad weather, he had decided to cut it down. Now, with the growth of new shoots from the old branches, the tree could be saved. This was one of the most fortunate decisions Jesse Hiatt ever made. It also proved important to those who enjoy fine fruits.

When autumn came, the tree bore ripe fruit, but the apples were so unusual the Hiatt family felt they had to be no good. The apples appeared deformed. They were elongated, with a row of small nubs encircling the end opposite the stem.

However, the Hiatts tasted the apples and found that they had a sweetness and a different flavor than they had ever tasted in an apple before. Everyone agreed that the fruit was delicious.

Cuttings from the tree were rooted to create other trees of the same kind. During the next twelve years, Hiatt was active in improving this type of apple and in increasing the number of new trees. He began to market his apple commercially, calling it the Hawkeye in honor of the Hawkeye State.

In 1894 Hiatt sold the rights to the fruit to Stark Brothers Nurseries and Orchards. They introduced the new apple on a wide commercial scale. Since everyone thought the apples were delicious, Starks decided to call them Delicious apples. They felt this name would become so valuable that they even took out a trademark on it.

Opposite: The original Delicious apple tree roots have produced these sturdy offshoots—firmly rooted in Iowa soil near Peru.

In 1907, Secretary of Agriculture James (Tama Jim) Wilson, who was an Iowan, called it a "promising new fruit."

All of them were right about the name and the popularity of the new apple. In a comparatively few years the Delicious apple became known and loved nationwide.

The millions of Delicious apple trees that have been grown since and the millions of bushels of Delicious apples that have enriched the bank accounts of orchard owners and delighted apple eaters around the world all are direct descendants of that one apple tree in Hiatt's Iowa orchard.

The main cultivation of the Delicious apple came in other states, but the original Iowa tree might be considered one of the most famous and unusual trees in history, and it lived on until the blizzard of 1942.

But this hardy old Iowa pioneer was not through yet. Two years later, shoots began to sprout from the roots, and today near Peru two full-grown offshoots of the original may still be seen, protected by an iron fence. The old tree continues to perpetuate itself and its story.

This is a unique series of events, but it is only one of the many enchanting stories of Iowa, a state which has given the world so many other delightful foods.

Lay of the Land

"It is worthless country," sadly declared some of the first Europeans to visit what is now Iowa. They thought its level treeless lands were without value. There seemed to be no mineral riches and few timberlands.

And yet the land between the two great rivers probably has the richest treasure given by nature to any state. Unlike gold or other important minerals, this great wealth is difficult to appreciate.

The incredible fortune of Iowa comes through its possession of one-fourth of all the grade A land in the United States. From this treasure comes a far greater production of food than from any similar region in the world.

For the most part, Iowa's rich soils were brought in from other regions by the glaciers that covered various parts of the state at four different times; but the northeast region had only one ice mantle. This kept the heavy ice from scraping off the hills and filling in valleys as it did in other parts. Because of this, the northeast region is rougher and more hilly and now bears the title Little Switzerland.

Before the glaciers, many millions of years ago, Iowa was covered by shallow seas, not once but several times. Numerous types of minerals were formed from the compressed remains of plants and animals that flourished in the seas and then died. Coal deposits and limestone were formed in this way.

Today, the landscape of Iowa is beautifully gentle. Bluffs along many rivers provide scenic lookouts. Most of the rivers are bordered by heavily wooded areas of hardwood trees that turn to spectacular color during the fall.

Iowa is the only state with two principal navigable rivers forming its boundaries. The Mississippi River makes up the entire eastern boundary. Two-thirds of the western border is traced by the mighty Missouri River. The Big Sioux River cuts along the remainder of the western boundary. Altogether, Iowa has 600 miles (966 kilometers) of boundary streams.

The Cedar and Des Moines rivers are both on the list of the U.S. Geological Survey's major rivers of the United States. Other impor-

Most Iowa rivers are bordered by heavily wooded areas of hardwood trees that turn to spectacular color during the fall.

tant rivers are the Iowa, Wapsipinicon, Skunk, Raccoon, and Little Sioux.

Iowa now contains about a hundred lakes, many of which are artificial. The state creates additional lakes by damming streams in order to conserve the water and the land and to provide greater recreation facilities. Okiboji and Spirit lakes are the largest natural bodies of water in Iowa.

Lake Okiboji has been called the third most beautiful lake in the world by the National Geographic Society.

Wall Lake is an unusual body of water. It freezes solid almost every winter. The ice pushes boulders on the bottom toward the shores. Through the years, this movement has formed a wall of boulders around the shore, giving the lake its name.

Strangely enough, the highest point in Iowa is a man-made hill— Ocheyedan Mound, formed of dirt piled high by prehistoric men.

12

Footsteps on the Land

SPIRIT PLACES AND PEOPLE OF THE GREAT SPIRIT

The only national park or national monument in Iowa is Effigy Mounds National Monument, near McGregor. The United States government has set aside a group of curiously shaped heaps of dirt to be preserved forever as a part of our national heritage. It is apparent that these earth mounds must once have been significant.

When viewed from above, some of these mounds appear to be formed in the shape of animals or birds, which means they must have been made by intelligent people. Many thousands of years ago the prehistoric men and women who lived in what is now Iowa built these and many other mounds.

*Snow helps to outline this bird effigy
at Effigy Mounds National Monument.*

The mounds were made for several reasons. Some were used for burying the dead. Others might have had wooden temples or other buildings constructed on their tops. Some served as fortifications.

At least six different groups of people lived in Iowa before any written records were kept. Without such records, all information about these peoples must be gathered from the few materials that have been unearthed over the years.

The artifacts left by prehistoric Iowa people are fascinating to archaeologists and laymen alike. The presence of these people is recalled by such things as shell heaps, cemeteries, and carvings. The prehistoric peoples have left traces of their trails, their spirit places, and even their fish traps. Some village sites can be marked out, and paintings have been found on rocks. Further discoveries will result in more knowledge about Iowa's ancient peoples.

The Indians who lived in Iowa when the first Europeans arrived knew nothing about the prehistoric people who may have been their ancestors. These Indians were divided, generally, into two large groups—the Plains Indians and the Woodland Indians.

The Plains Indians had occupied the region for a longer time period. They fought the coming of the Woodland Indians, who had been pushed farther and farther west by the Iroquois and the European settlers.

The Ioway, Osage, Winnebago, Missouri, Ponca, Omaha, Wahpeton, and Sisseton tribes were among the Plains Indians found in Iowa. Woodland tribes included the Illini, Fox, Sauk, Chippewa (sometimes called Ojibway), Potawatomi, Ottawa, and Miami.

The Ioway, who are generally thought to have given the state its name, never numbered more than about fifteen hundred. Although the Ioway were strong warriors, most of them were killed in wars with the Sauk and Fox Indians.

As the settlers pushed farther west, the Indians who were driven out also moved into the western lands of their Indian neighbors, causing much hardship on all sides. Then, as the newcomers continued to move in without letup, the Indians were again forced from their homes.

In 1848 the United States government decided to move the entire

Rolling Prairie, Iowa. *Painting by Henry Lewis.*

Winnebago tribe to new territory in Minnesota. The long caravan stretched out over the prairie as far as the eye could see. The group included 2,800 Indians—men, women, children, and infants hung in carrying saddles over the sides of the ponies—165 supply wagons, 143 cattle, 100 U.S. cavalrymen, and 2 lumbering cannon pulled by oxen.

Because of the forced eviction from their homes, the Indians were in an ugly mood. Braves would dash ahead, hide in the bushes, and take pot shots at the troops as they came up. At one time the whole group squatted on the ground and refused to move for five days.

When the caravan reached the Mississippi River not far from Fort Snelling, friendly Indians warned Captain Morgan, the commander, that the Winnebago chiefs were plotting with a wandering band of Sioux to massacre the whole force. Reinforcements were called for

from Fort Snelling—a nine-pound (four-kilogram) cannon, forty army regulars, and sixty friendly Sioux Indians.

All hands prepared for an attack. The covered wagons were run end-to-end in a semicircle with both ends touching the Mississippi. The troops barricaded this enclosure by rolling barrels of flour, pork, and beans against the wagon wheels on the inside.

Night brought a strange scene. Inside the enclosure the friendly Indians put on a war dance to display their fighting spirit. Meanwhile, the Indian women and troopers baked bread from soggy dough and cooked bacon over slow campfires. The sentries listened for footsteps and chilled to the yells of defiance from the hills above.

At dawn the hostile braves dashed down the prairie, armed for battle. They were painted beyond recognition, splattered with red coloring and with their hair set up on end with red clay. When the cannon and guns proved too much for them, the Winnebago agreed to move on again in exchange for a few beef cattle.

Captain Morgan later chartered a steamboat, and after many boat trips, all the Winnebago had left their Iowa home.

Today, the only Indian tribe living in Iowa is the Mesquakie. They had left the state for Kansas, but were so lonesome for Iowa that many saved their government allotments and made arrangements to buy 3,600 acres (1,457 hectares) of Iowa land near Tama. Several hundred gave up their government allotments to return to their new land, where about five hundred now live.

The Mesquakie have a democratic tribal government, electing a council of managers with a chief.

WHEN LEAD LED

In the years before 1673, Iowa was a favorite hunting ground of the Indians. In that year a small fleet of canoes carrying Europeans and Indian guides glided silently down the Mississippi River.

Opposite: Keokuk (The Running Fox), *by George Catlin*

This was the famous exploration party of Father Jacques Marquette and Louis Jolliet. It must have been one of the great moments in history when the canoes passed from the mouth of the Wisconsin River into the mighty Mississippi for the first time. Across the Mississippi stand the bluffs above what is now McGregor. As far as is known these were the first Europeans to see Iowa.

While the canoes slid down the Mississippi for several days, the Indians may have been watching, but they gave no indication. The explorers grew more and more anxious as the days went by. They feared the Indians might be fierce and hostile to them.

At last, the party came ashore, determined to meet the local Indians no matter what happened. The first encounter of Indians and Europeans in Iowa took place on June 25, 1673, eight days after the party had first reached the upper Mississippi.

There is some disagreement about the first meeting place, but it was probably located near Oakville, close to the mouth of the Iowa River. The Indians treated the exploring party with great respect, preparing a huge feast of dog meat and other delicacies. The hosts, as a sign of honor, insisted on placing the food in the mouths of the guests, much to the visitors' discomfort.

The Indians were members of the Illini tribe, most of whom lived in what is now Illinois.

The French claimed Iowa, along with much other North American territory, as a result of their early explorations. However, more than a century passed during which the region went almost unnoticed by Europeans, except for a few such as Nicholas Perrot, Lahontan and Le Sueur, William Des Lisle, and Joseph Des Noyelles.

These explorers traveled throughout much of Iowa. Perrot hunted for buffalo with the Indians; he also taught them how to mine lead in the area of Dubuque. Des Lisle mapped a trail completely across the northern section of Iowa, from the Mississippi to the Big Sioux. Des Noyelles led a force of eighty French soldiers and friendly Indians in battle against the Fox and Sauk in 1735, at the junction of the Raccoon and Des Moines rivers.

In 1762 France turned over to Spain the whole territory of Louisiana, including Iowa.

Dubuque, Iowa. *Painting by Henry Lewis.*

The Spanish hold on the Iowa portion of this land was never strong. They gave only three land grants during the period they held title to the region. One of these was to Julien Dubuque in 1796. He was the only permanent settler during the time of Spain's control.

Dubuque established himself at the mouth of Catfish Creek in 1788 and lived there until he died in 1810. His main occupation was lead mining. He had a great genius for getting along with the Indians, who called him their brother, Little Night.

On one occasion, Dubuque wanted a favor of some of the Fox Indians, but they refused. The French-Canadian vowed that he would burn up the Mississippi if he failed to get his way. When the Indians refused to believe he could carry out his threat, he invited them to see for themselves.

It was a strange gathering about the council fires at Catfish Creek. Dubuque had instructed one of his helpers hiding upstream to pour a barrel of oil into the creek. As the oil floated down, Dubuque seized a burning stick from the fire and thrust it into the creek. The whole area seemed to burst into flame.

Instantly the frightened Indians agreed to Dubuque's demands and asked him to put out the fire. He agreed just as the fire burned itself out. Dubuque's "great power and magic" were even more respected after this demonstration.

At Dubuque's death, the Indians argued with one another about who would have the honor of bearing his body to the grave.

BEES AND BOUNDARIES

In 1800 Spain secretly returned the Louisiana Territory—with Iowa—to France, and in 1803 Napoleon of France sold the entire vast area to the United States for $15 million.

No one knew just what the United States had bought or even exactly where some of the boundaries might be. The government therefore sent out a group of men to investigate, and their journey has become one of the most famous in the history of exploration. This was the Lewis and Clark expedition.

Lewis and Clark spent thirty-three days passing along the borders of what is now the state of Iowa, on the Missouri River. When they reached the present location of Sioux City, a member of the party, Sergeant Charles Floyd, died and was buried there. Sergeant Floyd was the only man of the Lewis and Clark expedition to die during the difficult and dangerous journey.

Another famous explorer, Zebulon Pike, pushed up the Mississippi and raised the first American flag in eastern Iowa in 1805, at the present site of Burlington. He gave his name to a bluff near McGregor, and although the Iowa Pike's Peak is much lower than the one in Colorado, it is still a notable landmark on the Mississippi.

Lieutenant Albert Lea helped put the name Iowa on the map. He explored the Iowa country, especially the valley of the Des Moines River, and used the name Iowa in his writing.

In 1808 the first American military post was established at Fort Madison, but it was evacuated and burned in 1813. During the War of 1812, the British controlled most of the upper Mississippi Valley.

Iowa was without organized government in 1821 when Missouri became a state. Iowa had been a part of Missouri Territory. However, although a few settlers lived in the region, there had been little need for government.

It seems strange that even before Iowa was settled, the first steamboat, the *Western Engineer,* pushed up the Missouri River as far as Council Bluffs in 1819, just fifteen years after Lewis and Clark had struggled so long against the swirling currents of that same river. Oddly enough, a steamboat did not reach the upper part of the Mississippi until 1823.

Western Engineer at Council Bluffs. *Sketch by Titian Peale. This was the first steamboat to push up the Missouri River as far as Council Bluffs.*

1824 painting of Mahaskah, or White Cloud, by Charles Bird King.

The first permanent legal settlement in Iowa was founded in 1833. This was possible because the defeat of the Indians in the Black Hawk War led to the release of Iowa land previously held by the Indians, and settlers were officially permitted to come in.

One year later, Iowa became a part of the territory of Michigan, and in 1836 it was annexed to the newly formed territory of Wisconsin. For a short time, Burlington, in Iowa, was the capital of Wisconsin Territory. A separate Iowa Territory was formed in 1838, with Robert Lucas as governor.

The new territory had scarcely been established before Iowa and Missouri began to quarrel about their common boundary. This dispute grew into what is known as the Honey War.

The Iowa-Missouri boundary was to run westward from the "rapids of the River Des Moines." Iowans thought this meant the

Des Moines rapids in the Mississippi, but Missouri claimed it meant a small rapids in the Des Moines River, 13 miles (21 kilometers) farther north. The Missouri claim would have stripped Iowa of almost 2,600 square miles (6,734 square kilometers) of territory.

More important for the pioneers, this territory contained some of the finest bee trees anywhere. The honey provided by the bees in these trees was of great value to the early settlers.

When Sandy Gregory, sheriff of Clark County, Missouri, came into Van Buren County to collect Missouri's taxes on the disputed land, a crowd of Iowans kidnapped him and held him prisoner. Missouri Governor Lilburn Boggs immediately called out his militia to go to the sheriff's rescue, and some Missouri men retaliated for the kidnapping by slipping over the "border" and cutting down three of the prized honey trees.

Governor Lucas of the Iowa Territory mustered out his militia, and Iowa's "army" marched for the border.

They formed a strange group. Each man chose his uniform according to his own taste, and almost no one had a gun. One man cut out a sword from a piece of sheet iron; another used the coulter from a plow for his weapon. Still another found the dasher from a churn to be the only weapon available. Numerous pitchforks were among the most dangerous weapons on both sides.

One captain purchased six wagon loads of supplies to make his men happy; five of the wagons were loaded with liquor.

Troops from both sides straggled up to the disputed border, but the call to fight never came, because both governors appointed a committee to settle the dispute. However, it dragged on until settled in Iowa's favor in 1850 by the United States Supreme Court.

One woman who owned property in the disputed no-man's-land said she was grateful her land was going to remain in Iowa, because she had heard the Missouri climate was not very good for crops.

Regular church services in Iowa were first begun by the Reverend Barton Randle, a Methodist minister, at Dubuque in 1833. Since there was no church building in all of Iowa, Mr. Randle held services in a tavern. In 1834 the people of Dubuque contributed funds for the state's first church building. Almost everyone in the pioneer community helped erect the log building, which measured only twenty-six feet (eight meters) long, twenty feet (six meters) wide, and ten feet (three meters) high.

This first church building in Iowa was used by all congregations—even, after some dispute, by a Mormon missionary. But most of the services were held by Methodists. Regularly the twelve members of the first Iowa Methodist congregation went to Sunday school, class meeting, prayer meeting, preaching service, and quarterly conference in its bare interior.

The Reverend Mr. Randle stayed in Dubuque for a year, then moved on. He had received $100 for his year's work. The church later was used on weekdays as a public school. In 1839 a new church at Dubuque replaced the first structure.

Very shortly after Mr. Randle arrived in Dubque, Father Samuel Charles Mazzuchelli came to that frontier city. The brilliant young priest soon won the respect of everyone.

Father Mazzuchelli made plans for St. Raphael's Church at Dubuque and helped spread the mortar with his own hands. He designed and drew plans for Iowa's most famous and beautiful building, the Old Stone Capitol at Iowa City.

"Father Matthew Kelly," as Father Mazzuchelli's Irish friends liked to call him, established and planned more than twenty Catholic churches in Iowa. In 1864 he died of pneumonia brought on by over-exposure in caring for the sick.

Only four years after Father Mazzuchelli came to Dubuque, the community had grown so that the See of Dubuque could be created in 1837, and the first Catholic Bishop of Iowa, Mathias Loras, took over his diocese of thirty-one hundred members in 1839. Loras College at Dubuque bears his name.

George C. Duffield, in an interesting account in the *Annals of Iowa,* tells of the first Presbyterian service in the state. The service was held in 1837, on the banks of the Des Moines River, under a huge elm on the former Duffield farm. After the minister had delivered his "burning" two-hour sermon, Duffield felt "sure young people in general, and I in particular, were but a few inches above the rotten ridge pole in the burning pit."

24

When the Reverend Asa Turner came to Denmark, Iowa, in the late 1830s, he found three small cabins and a schoolhouse. Sometimes as many as eighteen people had to sleep in a single one-room cabin. Nevertheless, the year he arrived Mr. Turner established at Denmark the first Congregational church west of the Alleghenies. Within fifteen years, Denmark Academy, sponsored by the church, was flourishing with an enrollment of 104 students in a $4,000 building constructed entirely by the people of the little community.

The story is told about the first road in Iowa. Since there were few trees on which to blaze a trail, and no roads on the Iowa prairies, many pioneer families became lost, often for days. Lyman Dillon, a Dubuque merchant, decided to do something about it.

He hitched his five oxen to a heavy plow and plowed a deep, straight furrow all the way to Iowa City, quite possibly the longest continuous furrow ever plowed. Soon a well-worn wagon road ran beside Dillon's furrow. Today a concrete highway follows almost exactly the same route.

During the short thirteen years between the first permanent settlement in Iowa and the year 1846, the population mushroomed to the almost unbelievable figure of 102,388.

Iowa very definitely was ready for statehood, and so on December 28, 1846, Iowa became the first free state admitted to the Union from the Louisiana Purchase. Ansel Briggs took office as the first governor. George W. Jones and A.C. Dodge served as Iowa's first United States senators.

In 1854 a crude, iron-bound wooden girder was swung out on a derrick, dropped slowly down, and touched both ends of an unfinished bridge. For the first time in history, the Mississippi River had been bridged.

Yesterday and Today

BETWEEN TWO WARS

The new state of Iowa became involved in the nation's problems almost immediately. During the year Iowa became a state, the United States went to war with Mexico. Lieutenant Benjamin S. Roberts of Fort Madison led the assault at far-off Chapultepec.

Civilization moved quickly into Iowa after statehood. The telegraph lines came into the state in 1848, and the first railroad was begun in 1853.

The railroad company had brought in two thousand Irish workers from New York to build the road; the company then ran out of money to pay their wages. Instead of cash the workers began to receive food and dry goods from the company stores. So many bolts of cloth were given out that the road is still sarcastically called The Calico Road.

Before the railroad was finished a very important problem remained unsolved. There was no locomotive, and without a bridge across the Mississippi no one could figure out a way to bring an engine over the river to run on the new railroad. One night the chief engineer of the railroad, a Mr. Slack, went to bed after thinking hard about the problem; he had a nightmare. He dreamed that he was being chased across the Mississippi by a runaway locomotive and that both he and the locomotive were jumping from one cake of ice in the river to another.

In the morning Slack decided that a locomotive could be slid across the Mississippi on the ice during the coldest weather. And the first locomotive was brought into the state in 1854 in just that way.

The Rock Island Railroad reached Iowa City from Davenport on January 1, 1856. The celebration in honor of the first train ever to reach Iowa City was the biggest in the history of the old capital. Every window in the town had a candle to light up the streets. The capitol building was lit from top to bottom with forty-three hundred candles. At last Iowa had fifty miles (eighty kilometers) of railroad.

Meanwhile, workers had finished one of the great construction projects of the pioneer period. In 1854 a crude, iron-bound wooden girder was swung out on a derrick, with great ceremony. Crowds watched from both banks as the girder dropped slowly down and touched both ends of an unfinished bridge. Shouts went up from the Davenport and Rock Island shores. For the first time in history, the mighty Mississippi River had been bridged.

By 1856 the bridge was completed and a railroad train passed over and sped into Iowa, the first crossing of the Mississippi by bridge. The new link stretched 1,580 feet (482 meters) across the Father of Waters; its total cost of $400,000 was enormous for that time, and the people of Iowa were justly proud. To ensure navigation for larger boats, the central span swung out by means of complicated machinery, a triumph of engineering.

Iowa needed the bridge. Thousands of new settlers crossed over it into Iowa in 1856. The people of St. Louis were furious. The city's businessmen had visions of the rich trade between East and West all being routed over the bridge and through Chicago. They formed "stop the bridge" clubs. New Orleans also took up the fight, calling the new bridge a "work of the devil."

The two cities brought suit in federal court, and the case dragged on. A steamer bumped into the middle pier of the bridge, and both the boat and the western section of the bridge went up in smoke. But Davenport and Rock Island sent out building crews that quickly repaired the bridge.

In 1859 lawyer Abraham Lincoln pleaded before the court that construction of the bridge was entirely within the law. Shortly thereafter, on a dark night, the night watchman at the bridge saw dark forms quietly creeping about on the central span. When he hurried out, four men clambered down the iron work of the pier and escaped in a boat. Several hundred pounds of inflammable and explosive material had been piled on the wooden floor of the bridge.

Feeling ran high. Davenport accused St. Louis of trying to destroy the bridge, but this could not be proved. The bridge continued to carry goods and people safely across the Mississippi into the promised land of Iowa.

The old bridge has been replaced by newer and better spans, but it played an important part in the building of the state.

The year 1854 also saw the opening of the first state fair, held at Fairfield. The University of Iowa in Iowa City began to operate on a very small scale in 1855. At that same time a group of German immigrants founded a cooperative community called Amana, a name later known around the world.

In 1856 the young town of Des Moines became the state capital. A year later the governorship was captured by the even younger

Iowa's Amana colonies are probably the most successful cooperative settlement in history. Though not cooperative today, the Amana enterprises flourish and are known all over the world. The seven communities founded in 1856 draw large numbers of visitors, attracted to the "simple country life" and the record of its success, as well as its splendid food and locally made products.

Republican Party. Ralph P. Lowe was the first in what became an almost unbroken succession of Iowa Republican governors.

Iowa had turned Republican because so many citizens believed that the older Democratic Party was the party of slavery, and this great problem was dividing the American people as no other issue before in the nation's short existence. The well-known opponent of slavery, John Brown, had drilled some of his abolitionist followers at Springdale and Tabor.

Many Iowans actively helped in operating the Underground Railroad. This was a chain of locations, generally private homes, where escaped slaves could be hidden during the day. The slaves were cared for by sympathetic residents and then helped on during darkness to the next station on the road to safety in Canada.

The man who was to be a key figure in the growing dispute over slavery, Abraham Lincoln, came to Iowa in 1859. This was a year before he was elected to the presidency of the United States.

The Lincoln party visited Fairview Heights at Council Bluffs. Lincoln asked many questions about the area, perhaps already charting in his mind the course of a great transcontinental railroad. Talking to a friend in Council Bluffs on the last day of his stay, Lincoln suddenly pulled from his pocket a small package wrapped in an old newspaper. It was a United States land warrant for 160 acres (65 hectares) of Iowa land, given to him on his discharge after serving in the Black Hawk War.

He said he had been too poor to claim the land and pay taxes, but had kept the warrant to give his boys as a reminder that their father had been a soldier. That, he felt, was the only reason anyone would ever remember him. Later, Lincoln was able to claim another parcel of Iowa land, which remained in the Lincoln family until 1892.

EVEN THE GREYBEARDS FOUGHT

When the Civil War finally erupted, a Southern planter wrote to a Burlington merchant: "How many of the people of your town are in sympathy with this northern crusade on the South? We purchasers

30

of your dry goods are interested in knowing." The merchant replied by sending a copy of the town directory. His reply was a good index of Iowa loyalty that day in 1861 when Fort Sumter fell.

Each state was expected to arm and equip its own troops for the Civil War, but as a result of the depression of 1857, financial conditions in Iowa were poor. Banks had failed, and many businesses were in trouble. Thousands of volunteers were pouring in, expecting uniforms and arms.

At his own expense, Iowa Governor Samuel J. Kirkwood outfitted the entire First Regiment. Women throughout Iowa donated their services to make the uniforms. Banks from every part of the state wired messages such as "Draw on us for any amount necessary." Hundreds of private homes quartered soldiers without pay.

Finally the First Iowa Regiment was outfitted and ready to leave by boat for the battlefront.

"As the *Kate Cassell* moved off," recalls the *Burlington Hawkeye,* "cheer after cheer broke forth again, mingled with the cries of the wives and mothers."

Iowa troops played particularly important roles in the battles of Wilson's Creek, Iuka, Shiloh, Corinth, the siege of Vicksburg, and Sherman's March to the Sea.

The Battle of Iuka in September 1862, it has been written, "made Iowa famous in war annals." General Price's Confederate forces had only to defeat General William Rosecrans at Iuka in northwest Mississippi to weaken the Northern army so much that all the northwest Union states might have fallen into Southern hands.

When Price charged, the Fifth Iowa Infantry, under Colonel Matthies, was thrown across the road directly in the Southerners' path. S.H.M. Byers, the distinguished Iowa war historian, a soldier of the Fifth at Iuka, tells of the battle: "We fixed our sword bayonets on our good Whitney rifles and sat down to wait the coming foe. Nearer they come. We hear their very tramp.

"We think of Iowa. She shall not be dishonored; rather every man at Iuka die than that. The Texans, Louisianians and the Mississippians, veterans of bloody fields, find that out and falter in the blast from our guns.

Iowa troops played a key role in the Battle of Wilson's Creek in nearby Missouri. Federal General Nathaniel Lyon lost his life, as shown in this old Kurz and Allison print, along with nearly a fourth of his troops, but the battle so weakened the Southern forces that Missouri was saved for the Union. In reporting the battle one newspaper stated: "Some of the best blood in the land was being spilled as recklessly as if it were ditch water; on few other fields was there a greater display of courage and bravery."

"Blood crimsons the grass and leaves. Poor Shelby of Jasper fell first. We only close up, touch elbows and with grim faces fire and fire until we in turn shall drop in the leaves and blood of that afternoon. No man of the Fifth yields a foot of ground.

"A big red-shirted Alabamian breaks through the ranks and attempts to seize the colors of the Fifth but is bayoneted. At the range of but a few feet, the lines fire volleys in each other's faces.

"So the regiment fought until the sun went down; darkness settled on the battlefield, and Price prepared to bury the dead and retreat before the dawn of the morrow."

All that night doctors crept about the field with candles, tending the wounded. The field hospital was filled. Two hundred seventeen of the Fifth Iowa were dead or wounded. "It was the hardest fought battle I ever witnessed," wrote General Price.

As a tribute to the Hawkeye State, General Rosecrans's official report declared: "Iowa men held the post of danger and honor throughout the battle."

In 1863 Iowa had more men on the battlefield than George Washington ever commanded at one time. The Iowa recruiting offices had sent home a thousand boys who were far too young to enlist. However, some of them later enlisted by falsifying their age. The draft had never been used in Iowa, for the state was twelve thousand men ahead of its quota.

In spite of all these volunteers from Iowa, demands to join the army kept pouring in from older men all over the state. Finally, Governor Kirkwood received special permission from the United States Secretary of War to form a regiment of men over the legal age of forty-five.

The regiment was soon mustered and left for St. Louis, where the soldiers' snappy step and smart appearance were much admired. Many of the Iowa men were more than seventy years old, most of them older than fifty. They came to be known as the Greybeard Regiment.

The Greybeards enlisted even though 1,300 of their sons and grandsons were on the fighting front. The men were not expected to fight, but were given duties of escorting trains and guarding railroads and prisoners. A supply train which they were guarding near Memphis was fired on by the Confederates; two Greybeards were killed, but the rest got the train through. During their service, they guarded more than 160,000 Southern prisoners.

In recognition of their services, the Greybeards were mustered out at Davenport in 1865, the first group of three-year men anywhere in the country to be honorably discharged.

Iowa women served the war effort in many ways. "No soldier on the firing line ever gave more heroic service than Annie Wittenmyer rendered," said General U.S. Grant when the last of the Wittenmyer diet kitchens was disbanded in 1865.

Mrs. Wittenmyer had been a leader in mobilizing the women of Iowa into a powerful organization that furnishished food, hospital supplies, clothing, and money for the Union Army's benefit.

One day Mrs. Wittenmyer visited her youngest brother, David Turner, a sixteen-year-old soldier who was sick in the military hospital at Sedalia, Missouri. It was breakfast time, and the attendant brought in the boy's tray. He waved it away feebly. "If you can't eat this you'll have to do without; there is nothing else," said the waiter, who marched off.

"On a dingy-looking wooden tray," wrote Mrs. Wittenmyer later, "was a tin cup full of black strong coffee; beside it was a leaden looking tin platter, on which was a piece of fried fat bacon, swimming in its own grease, and a slice of bread."

While she made her rounds distributing goods, doing errands for the wounded, and helping in all types of emergencies, Mrs. Wittenmyer tried to solve the problems of the soldiers' diet. Many patients needed a satisfactory diet more than medicine, but scientific dieticians were almost unknown in those days.

Mrs. Wittenmyer finally persuaded the government to establish special diet kitchens where two women prepared food for each patient according to the doctors' written orders. Mrs. Wittenmyer took charge of the supervision of these diet kitchens, and by the end of the war more than a hundred had been installed in various hospitals. This was something new in military history, and the Iowa woman became nationally famous.

Almost eighty thousand Iowa men took part in the Civil War. More than twelve thousand Iowans died or were killed in service.

MUCH TRUE AND SOME FALSE

After the Civil War, in 1867, the North Western Railroad was finished to Council Bluffs, becoming the first railroad to cross the entire state of Iowa. Two years later, the transcontinental railroad was completed, connecting with Council Bluffs as its eastern terminal. President Abraham Lincoln, remembering his visit to Council Bluffs, had chosen the terminal site before his death. The goods of an entire continent began to flow back and forth across Iowa.

The census of 1870 showed that 1,194,020 people were residents of Iowa, less than forty years after Iowa became a state.

In that same year an Iowa "man" became one of the most notorious subjects of his time. Some men were digging a well on the old Newall farm near the little town of Cardiff, New York, when they uncovered what seemed to be a man's foot. More digging revealed the stonelike body of a ten-foot (three-meter) giant.

As news of the find spread, visitors began to swarm to the farm. Newall and his cousin, George Hull, put up a fence and tent around the figure's resting places. In a short time they had taken in more than $20,000 in ten-cent admissions.

Scientists visited the tent and wrote learned volumes on the Cardiff Giant. Many, pointing to the tiny holes all over the body, which they called pores, said the giant was a petrified man. Others thought it might be a statue made by prehistoric men.

An Indian medicine man declared the giant was an old Indian prophet who foretold the coming of the Europeans and their later discovery of the prophet's own body. The medicine man even pointed out what looked like veins in the stone, saying that they followed the pattern of Indians' veins.

There was some suspicion that the object might not be genuine, but nothing could be proved. However, Galusha Parsons, a Fort Dodge lawyer, visited the statue one day. "Why," he said, "that's that big block of Fort Dodge gypsum those fellows shipped out of town last year."

George Hull admitted the fraud. While visiting in Ackley, Iowa, he had listened to a Methodist minister's sermon and got the idea of burying a lifelike statue, waiting a year or so, and then arranging for a "resurrection."

Hull had a 7,000-pound (3,175-kilogram) piece of gypsum quarried and had it shipped to Chicago. A sculptor there chiseled out the statue while Hull posed. Then they all went to work with steel needles and wooden mallets and made the "pores." Finally, the thing was shipped to New York State by a roundabout route, buried in the dead of night, and left to weather for a year; then the "discovery" took place.

And so Iowa played its key part in one of the most famous hoaxes of all times.

The original Cardiff Giant now is on display
at the Farmers Museum, Cooperstown, New York.

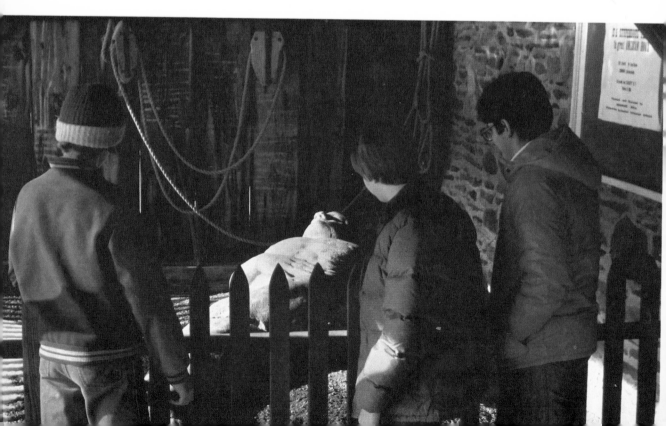

Early in 1876, two Englishmen, James and Fred Close, bought 30,000 acres (12,140 hectares) of land near Le Mars, Iowa. In a few years several hundred English people bought land in the Le Mars region and came to farm it. They were different from most of the Iowa pioneers. The English bought huge farms and hired men to work their farms while they lived the life of country gentlemen.

Almost every train brought men "who carried the latest agony in canes" and women "in the most coquettish of bonnets." They left the trains daintily and swept haughtily up the street, but the next day they would appear in corduroys and woolens ready for work. They were respected by all and survived all of the frontier's hardships.

The English who settled in Iowa are no longer a distinct group, but they brought a bit of cosmopolitan culture to the state.

The calm of a peaceful afternoon at Estherville in 1879 was shattered by a sizzling sound like an enormous skyrocket. A tremendous explosion shook the town and the region for fifty miles (eighty kilometers) around. Windows broke; dishes fell from their places. The Estherville meteor had arrived.

When it exploded, the meteor burst into three major pieces, each one flying in a different direction and each one showering the countryside with fragments of molten metal. At least three persons— Charles Ega, John Barber, and Mrs. Sever H. Lee—saw the heavenly visitor in the sky.

The largest piece carved a cone-shaped hole 15 feet (4.5 meters) deep and 12 feet (3.6 meters) wide at the top, splattering dirt and stones up around the edge like a volcano. Three men and a derrick were needed to drag this piece out of the ground. It was 27 inches (68 centimeters) long and weighed 431 pounds (195 kilograms).

The second piece, weighing about 150 pounds (68 kilograms), was sold to the museum of the University of Minnesota. The third piece was sold to Charles P. Birge of Keokuk, but its present location is unknown.

The largest piece was finally sold to the British Museum of Natural History, where it was sawed into three more pieces. Two of the pieces were sold to museums in Paris and Vienna.

No large pieces remained in Iowa. Small fragments, however,

were scattered over the fields for miles, and for several years meteor-hunting picnics were a common recreational activity. The local blacksmith was kept busy forging finger rings out of small lumps.

Nature again made news in Iowa on June 17, 1882. There had been severe storms all over the state that day, but the most severe began at the town of Kellogg, about ten miles (sixteen kilometers) from Grinnell. There two black clouds met and began to rotate, forming a tornado that moved northeast toward Grinnell.

Shortly before, another tornado had formed in Carroll County. It began to move southeast toward Grinnell.

In the very center of the town, the two tornadoes met with a terrible roar. From the huge cloud that formed, at least half a dozen tornadoes were seen to dart down to earth. One of these struck the college. The only college property saved was the college bell.

Thirty-nine persons were killed in the Grinnell tornado, and property damage was estimated at $250,000. It remains to this day one of the worst examples of such storms.

History of another kind was made in Iowa in 1889 when the University of Iowa and Grinnell College played the first intercollegiate football game west of the Mississippi. During the next few decades, the teams of Iowa State University at Ames and the University of Iowa at Iowa City became among the most powerful and famous in the nation. Some of the Iowa State players of the 1890s are still considered among the most outstanding of all time.

Although it seems strange now, Iowa in the 1890s also became an international center for another sport—horse racing. In 1885 Charles W. Williams, an Independence, Iowa, creamery man, bought two mares. When two colts came, he called them Axtell and Allerton and began patiently to train them.

As a yearling, Axtell could have been bought for $300, but nobody would have him. As a two-year-old, he established a new two-year-old trotting record. When three years old, he set records with regularity. Then Axtell established a new world trotting record for stallions of any age, and Williams sold him to a syndicate for $105,000.

38

In the meantime, Williams had been making Independence one of America's greatest racing centers. Williams established a racing newspaper, *The American Trotter,* which soon was more widely read than any other horseman's journal in the country.

Williams built and operated a three-story hotel and opera house at Independence in 1892. The floors were tiled. Parlors were finished in mahogany, carpeted with Axminster, and furnished beautifully.

Then Williams built a $40,000 electric trolley line from the railroad depot past his hotel and out to Rush Park, his racetrack. This track was the wonder of its day. Shaped like an odd figure eight, it became known as the "kite track" and was said to be several seconds faster than ordinary tracks.

Within the space of two short weeks in 1892, more records fell at Independence than at all the other tracks in the world during the same period.

Meanwhile, Allerton had been coming to the front. He conquered the champions Nelson, Delmarch, and McDoel and, as a five-year-old, was crowned the stallion champion of the world for doing a mile in 2:09¼. He lost only one important race, and that was to the grand mare, the famous Nancy Hanks.

When the depression of 1893 struck, Williams left Independence. In later years he sold all his horses and became an evangelist, preaching at Waterloo, Independence, and other towns.

Iowa's racing glory has faded, but Charles Williams is still remembered as the only man ever to develop two horses to hold the world's stallion trotting record.

As the century reached its end, matters much more serious occupied attention. When the United States battleship *Maine* was sunk in Havana Harbor in February 1898, feeling in Iowa against Spain ran high. One of the two officers killed was an Iowan, Darwin R. Merritt, of Red Oak. He was an assistant engineer of the ship.

Memorial services were held in Red Oak for the Annapolis graduate, and angry meetings throughout the state were held to demand revenge on the "assassins" of the Iowa man.

Iowa men in the Spanish-American War, all volunteers, served with distinction. When the Fifty-first Iowa Regiment left for the

Philippines in 1899, it became the first group of Iowa soldiers ever to cross the ocean to take part in battle.

Long after the war had ended, the *Maine* was raised, the lockers were opened, and the men's personal property was taken out. The Iowa Historical Library at Des Moines has preserved the trinkets taken from Darwin Merritt's locker on the *Maine*—a bunch of moldy keys, an old watch case, and the rusted hilt of a sword—Iowa's mementos of the deed that started the Spanish-American War.

A NEW CENTURY

With the coming of a new century, scientific and mechanical affairs took on increasing prominence in Iowa, as they did in many other areas. The automobile came into use during the first decade of the 1900s. Iowans marveled at the sight of a dirigible steering majestically around the capitol dome in 1906.

In 1912 the famous pioneer aviator Lincoln Beachey was sworn in by the Dubuque postmaster as a special postal clerk. He took off from the Dubuque fairgrounds with a sack of mail. After flying over the city, he swooped low and dropped the mail in front of a local hotel.

Two years later William "Billy" Robinson of Grinnell, one of Iowa's pioneer airmen, received permission from the United States government to fly mail from Des Moines to Chicago. Overshooting Chicago, he landed in Kentland, Indiana, averaging 80 miles (129 kilometers) an hour for the 362 miles (582 kilometers). This was not only the first overland air-mail flight, it also set a new cross-country nonstop distance record.

When the *Lusitania* was sunk in 1915 with a loss of almost a hundred American lives, Iowa became more acutely aware of the war raging in Europe. The state, however, was not thrown into a feverish war excitement. Many Iowans opposed American involvement in the politics of Europe.

When the United States entered the war on April 6, 1917, Iowa gave its usual all-out effort. With 2 percent of the nation's popula-

Iowa artist Grant Wood created this World War I memorial window for the Cedar Rapids Memorial Coliseum.

tion, Iowa suffered 5 percent of America's deaths in action in the first year of the war.

Merle Hay, an Iowa boy, was one of the first three Americans killed in the war.

An Iowa seaman, J.C. Sabin, is said to have fired America's first shot of the war. Sabin was a sailor on the armed transport *Jupiter*. Not far from French shores, the *Jupiter* sighted two German submarines. The gun crew flew into action and when the range was found, Sabin fired.

After keeping up the fire for some time, Sabin's crew sank one of the subs. The other escaped. The United States had won its first encounter of the war.

Some 114,000 Iowans took an active part in World War I, and Iowa mourned the state's 3,576 war dead. The government's war heroes list, issued in 1919, contained 205 Iowa men who received medals for distinguished service at the front.

In the late 1930s the University of Iowa football team gained national fame as the "Iron Men." Iron man Nile Kinnick (right) won the Heisman trophy in 1939.

After the war, Iowa began many improvements. A state park system was established and the state's attention turned to the condition of its roads. Iowa possessed only 586 miles (943 kilometers) of paved roads in 1925. The 75-mile (121-kilometer) stretch from Algona to Charles City was the longest single run of paving anywhere in the state. In the short space of ten years, Iowa jumped to rank fourth in the country in paving mileage.

During the early 1930s the Great Depression came to Iowa. By 1932, especially in western Iowa, drought, hail, and insect pests had brought three years of virtually no crops. Money was so scarce that farmers began exchanging their products with one another instead of trying to buy goods with money.

Because of the depression, the Republican hold on state government ended in 1932, and the Democrats gained complete control of Iowa government for the first time since before the Civil War. Six years later, the Republicans were swept back into power once more.

In 1941, for the second time in less than twenty-five years, the United States once again entered a world war. More than 260,000 Iowans were members of the armed services during World War II, and 8,398 Iowans lost their lives as a result of the war.

Despite its agricultural leadership, by the 1960s Iowa had more people living in cities and towns than on farms.

In 1973 full adult rights were given to those who had reached eighteen years of age. In the mid-1970s the legislature worked on the revision of the state's criminal code, which had not been changed since statehood.

During the 1970s the state turned increasingly toward the Democratic party. The election of 1976 brought a Democratic majority to both houses of the legislature. However, popular long-time Governor Robert Ray retained his post.

Although there are no large cities in Iowa, the whole countryside has become in effect one vast city. Almost universal use of the automobile gives the Iowan complete access to both rural and urban ways of life. Iowans have been leaders in reversing the nation's trend toward the cities and in building new values into small town and country living. At the same time, the quality of life in the cities has been sweepingly improved. No longer isolated by their location, due to modern communications, Iowa people like to claim that they have the best of both worlds—rural and urban. They have all the advantages cities can give, such as fine schools, hospitals, clubs, and cultural activities, but also the knowledge gained by closeness to rural life—experiences which have been lost to much of the rest of the country.

A red-tailed hawk eyes the Hawkeye State.

Natural Treasures

The great wealth of Iowa, of course, is in the productivity of its soil.

Beneath the soil, large quantities of gypsum, cement materials, stone, sand, gravel and mica, and considerable coal are found.

No vast forests blanket the state to provide great income from lumbering, but farm wood lots and small lumber operations have been important to many residents. Since the 1930s, millions of trees have been planted in Iowa to provide wood, beauty, and shade and to form windbreaks against soil erosion.

Iowa was always a favorite hunting ground of the Indians. Buffalo and smaller game provided a livelihood for the Indian family. Today the buffalo are gone, but the small game still abounds. At present the state maintains public hunting grounds for both waterfowl and game.

Over what is called the Mississippi Flyway, some of the greatest flocks of waterfowl travel along the Iowa border to and from their winter and summer homes.

A bird originally imported from the Orient—the pheasant—has flourished in its faraway new home. Iowa's expanding pheasant population attracts a growing number of hunters.

The State Conservation Commission also provides wildlife refuges to protect scarce birds and animals and ensure their continuation.

One of the most precious resources of any state is its fresh water. Iowa was the most easterly state to adopt a comprehensive water rights law.

Protecting its wealth of fertile soil is one of Iowa's principal concerns. The State Soil Conservation Commission encourages and promotes soil conservation. Iowa's farmers generally have taken great pains to study the conservation of their land, using the most accepted methods of fertilization, crop rotation, contour plowing, watershed protection, and other effective measures so that one of the world's great treasures can be passed on from generation to generation.

People Use Their Treasures

YOUNG MACDONALD

Iowa is the "bread basket of the United States." Although half of the states are larger in area, Iowa produces a mammoth 10 percent of all the nation's food. The cash market value of agricultural products in Iowa each year is about $7 billion. Only California has a larger total, but California is almost three times as large as Iowa, and many of California's crops are of the high-priced specialty types.

Iowa usually is the world's greatest corn producer. It leads the country in value of livestock income. The state also has the largest hog production, accounting for 24 percent of the nation's hogs. Iowa pork production almost equals that of the next two states combined.

Iowa is foremost in chicken production and a leader in poultry production of all kinds, as well as eggs.

The state usually ranks first or second in oat, soybean, and popcorn production. Odeboldt is known as the "popcorn center of the world."

In 1952 Iowa became the first state to produce a single crop worth a billion dollars in one year's harvest, when the value of its corn pushed above that figure.

Iowa also produces other agricultural commodities. Southwestern Iowa, in the region of Shenandoah, is a leader in the growing of flowers for seeds. The region around Muscatine is a leading producer of melons, and the Muscatine melons are noted for their quality.

Long known as the Tall Corn State, Iowa naturally holds the record for the world's tallest corn stalk. In 1946 Don Radda of Washington grew a plant to the incredible height of 31 feet 3 inches (9.5 meters). Now corn "fashions" have changed, and tall corn is no longer desirable.

Opposite: Corn cob pile and a crib with a United States flag on the side symbolize Iowa, long called the Tall Corn State.

*Farmland in
Iowa, the
breadbasket
of the
United States.*

FACTORIES BESIDE THE FARMS

Iowa not only has given the world agricultural leadership but also has provided the most important machine used by farmers today.

In the early 1900s Charles W. Hart and Charles Parr of Charles City were experimenting with a means of putting their stationary gas engines on wheels to make a machine that would help the farmer with his work.

Since this was to be a type of "traction" machine, they invented a word to describe their device—tractor. That, of course, has been the word used ever since to describe such an implement.

The two men formed the Hart-Parr Company, and it has been a leading producer of tractors ever since. Another Iowa tractor works, by far the world's largest, is the John Deere plant at Waterloo.

Most people are surprised to learn that Iowa has many important manufacturing industries. In fact, the value of manufactured goods now nearly equals that of agricultural commodities. Many factories are located in the smaller cities and towns; in numerous cases factories and farms are side by side. Some farmers work part-time in manufacturing while many factory workers and executives operate farms. Des Moines, Cedar Rapids, Waterloo, and Dubuque are Iowa's leading industrial cities.

One of Iowa's most unusual activities, the freshwater pearl button industry, began in Muscatine in 1891. The story is told that John F. Boepple cut his foot on a clam shell while wading in the Mississippi River, and after this accident he started thinking of a way to put the plentiful clams to use.

Whether or not the story is true, Boepple began to manufacture buttons from the Mississippi clam shells, and the industry became the largest of its kind anywhere. Fleets of clammers operated on the river, and sometimes a lucky clammer found a freshwater pearl.

Boepple invented the first machines for producing pearl buttons, and today Muscatine is still a leader in manufacturing button-making machinery. At one time the Iowa button industry produced three-fourths of all the pearl buttons of the world.

A surprising number of the nation's large manufacturing companies were founded in Iowa.

W.A. Sheaffer began to manufacture fountain pens at Fort Madison, and the Sheaffer company is among the world's largest pen manufacturers.

At Newton, in the early 1900s, Frederick L. Maytag originated a machine for washing clothes. He set up a plant to manufacture his washing machines and now the Maytag Company is ranked as the world's largest manufacturer of clothes washers. At one time Iowa produced half of all the washing machines manufactured in the United States. Newton calls itself the "washing machine center of the world."

John W. Rath started a small meat-packing plant at Waterloo. That plant grew to become the largest single packing plant in the country at one time.

The Lennox Company at Marshalltown is one of the world's largest manufacturers of warm-air heating equipment, and the Quaker Oats Plant at Cedar Rapids is the world's largest cereal plant.

Quaker products are known throughout the world. An amusing illustration of this is told about an Iowa man visiting Scotland, famous for its oatmeal. He was so delighted with his Scottish oatmeal breakfasts that he ordered a whole barrel of the same kind of oatmeal to be sent to his Iowa home. After some time, his barrel of oatmeal arrived from Scotland, bearing the label "Quaker Oats, made in Cedar Rapids, Iowa."

Among other large manufacturers originating in Iowa are the Collins Radio Company of Cedar Rapids, Viking Pump Company of Cedar Falls, and the original Amana Company of the Amana Colonies, makers of home freezers, refrigerators, and other products.

Many leading firms with headquarters in other states have established important branches in Iowa. Alcoa built the world's largest aluminum plate rolling mill at Bettendorf, and Du Pont the world's

Corporations such as Quaker Oats combine agriculture and industry.

largest cellophane plant at Clinton. Honeywell, Sylvania, Zenith, Firestone, Avco, Proctor and Gamble, and Bendix Aviation have important Iowa operations.

In addition, Iowa is proud of some of the more unusual industries that the State Development Agency lists as among the largest of their types. These include a popcorn processing plant, a processor of honey, a door and millwork factory, an iron specialties factory, a poultry equipment manufacturer, a producer of resistors, a manufacturer of aluminum nails, a lawnmower factory, and a producer of secondary nickel alloy.

The Murphy Calendar Company at Red Oak is one of the largest in the world.

Iowa's mineral industries, in order of value of production, are cement, stone, sand and gravel, and gypsum. The cement industry is centered at Mason City, and at one time the Mason City area produced one-fifth of all the nation's cement. Mason City is also headquarters for a large clay manufacturing industry, producing brick, tile, and other clayware.

The large gypsum industry at Fort Dodge depends on the enormous reserve of gypsum in the area, which is said to cover 40 square miles (104 square kilometers). Gypsum is used in the making of plaster and related products.

One of the greatest early industries in Iowa has declined. In the 1880s Clinton was one of the world's leading lumber producers. Logs from the great forests of Wisconsin and Minnesota were transported down the Mississippi to Clinton for processing. So much sawdust came from the sawmills that the swampy land around the city was filled in with it and large portions of the city were built on "sawdust" lots.

When the supply of timber began to dwindle, the Clinton mills became far less productive.

Today, machinery and food processing are Iowa's two leading industries. Insurance, publishing and printing, and railroads are among other important businesses. Iowa, surprisingly, ranks high in railroad mileage among the states, giving it a position greatly out of proportion to its size.

Herbert Clark Hoover portrait by Elmer W. Green.

Human Treasures

**IOWAN, ENGINEER, HUMANITARIAN,
PRESIDENT, EFFICIENCY EXPERT, AUTHOR**

Probably Iowa's most illustrious and distinguished native son is Herbert Clark Hoover. It was a milestone in history when he became the first president of the United States to be born west of the Mississippi, but few people realize that in addition to his presidency, Herbert Hoover had one of the most colorful, interesting, useful, and varied lives of any American.

During his boyhood at West Branch, Iowa, where he was born in 1874, Hoover seemed to be nothing more than a regular boy. However, shortly after he entered Stanford University in California, as the very first student ever to live in the dormitory, he became a student leader.

After graduating in geology, Hoover rushed off to Australia, where he turned Australian gold mines into profitable investments on the American pattern. Taking just enough time off to return to California to get married, Hoover and his bride hurried to China, where he put many Chinese mines back into production.

Caught in Tientsin by the Boxer uprising, Hoover built barricades, protected the water supply, and received his first experience in the emergency control and rationing of food.

The next few years saw the Hoovers in practically every part of the world: Russia, India, the East Indies, China, Japan, Burma, Italy, England, and the United States. They had houses on three continents and used ocean liners as commuters use ferryboats.

When war broke out in Europe in 1914, Hoover was in England. As head of the American Relief Committee there, he helped thousands of Americans in Europe return home. Then he directed the commission for the relief of the starving people of Belgium.

After America entered the war, Hoover took charge of the country's food, increasing production, keeping down consumption, and raising our food exports from 5 to 15 million tons (4.5 to 13.6 million metric tons) a year.

At West Branch, President Herbert Hoover's birthplace and final resting place, a thirty-three-acre site preserves the historic Hoover home and has a beautiful library and museum devoted to his life and work.

Later, as United States secretary of commerce under Harding and Coolidge, Hoover turned his efficiency methods to improving business and trade.

At last came the day for his inauguration as president. Uncle John Reeder, age ninety-three, of Tipton, Iowa, went all the way to Washington to hold the president's hat during the ceremony.

Fifty thousand people stood in chilling rain on March 4, 1929, watching the president as he took the oath of office and kissed a Bible, opened to the verse in Proverbs which reads: "Where there is no vision the people perish, but he that keepeth the law, happy is he."

Hoover was unjustly blamed for many of the economic problems during his administration, and he fell into low esteem. He was soundly defeated in his bid for a second term in 1932 by Franklin Delano Roosevelt.

In 1947 he became chairman of the Committee for Reorganization of the Executive Branch of the Federal Government, and in 1953 chairman of the second Committee on Reorganization. This committee discovered means through which the federal government might save billions of dollars by exercising greater efficiency. Unfortunately, most of the committee's recommendations were never carried out.

Hoover also founded the Hoover Library on War, Revolution and Peace at Stanford University, and in his later life he wrote his very extensive memoirs and other books of commentary on history and problems of the times.

On August 10, 1962, the aged former president was on hand at West Branch, Iowa, to dedicate the new $500,000 Herbert Hoover Presidential Library in his native town. In a speech on that occasion he called for a new Council of Free Nations to be formed to preserve the peace.

Hoover stayed active throughout his life. Although some historians and commentators still fault Hoover for his economic policy during the Great Depression, he is now viewed more favorably than in the past. He died in New York City in 1964 at age ninety.

TAMA JIM

No one else has ever served in presidents' cabinets for as long as James Wilson, a native of Scotland, who as a boy moved to the Iowa prairie where the town of Traer later sprang up. Wilson had the unique distinction of serving for sixteen years under three presidents— William McKinley, Theodore Roosevelt, and William Howard Taft. What is more unusual, he began his cabinet service in his sixties, an age when most people are thinking more about retirement than starting a completely new career.

55

Wilson had served with distinction in the Iowa legislature and was elected to Congress. When Wilson went to Washington from Traer in his home district in Tama County, there was another James Wilson from Iowa there. People began to call him "Tama Jim" to distinguish one from the other.

As United States secretary of agriculture, Tama Jim was one of the first to make the nation realize the farmer's importance in American life. One of his principal goals was to educate the American farmer in correct and scientific methods of farming. Wilson tried to increase production by every possible means. It is due mainly to his efforts that America is the most productive agricultural nation in the world and the major food supplier for many countries around the globe.

Wilson's biographer, E.V. Wilcox, called his annual reports "poetry wedded to patriotism." This is shown in quotations from some of his annual reports:

"All the gold mines of the entire world have not produced, since Columbus discovered America, a greater value of gold than the farmers of this country have produced in two years."

"Every sunset during the last five years has registered an increase of $3,400,000 in the value of farms in this country. . . . There never was a country so rich as this. There was never a country so prosperous. There was never a country so productive as this. There was never a country where labor was so richly rewarded. . . . There was never a country in which human beings lived so well. . . ."

Tama Jim encouraged the development of scientific agriculture. His agents did the first work of introducing to an area the natural enemies of various insect pests. His department devised the methods for putting into effect the conservation ideas of President Theodore Roosevelt. Wilson sent his staff all over the world to bring back new plants that might grow well in the United States. They introduced African durum wheat, increasing the country's yield 60 million bushels (21 million hectoliters) a year, new varieties of rice for the South, alfalfa from Arabia and Peru, and hundreds of varieties of fruits.

Wilson never kept his department's discoveries secret; they were given freely for the improvement of agriculture all over the world.

Left: Portrait of James (Tama Jim) Wilson by Frank Kinney.
Below: The historic "Farmhouse" at Iowa State University where Tama Jim developed the pattern for the nation's agriculture is now preserved as a shrine to farming.

Today, his work is more widely recognized abroad than it is in this country.

Russell Lord said, "Tama Jim served with high usefulness as secretary of agriculture until the age of seventy-eight. He was sixty-two when he first took the post. In a sixteen-year term of duty, unprecedented at the time, and never since equaled, he transformed the Department from a puny and almost disregarded arm of government into the strongest and farthest-reaching of its kind on earth."

WALLACE, WALLACE, AND WALLACE

Iowa's Wallace family has been one of the few from the state to produce nationally prominent members for three generations.

The founder of the family in Iowa, the first Henry Wallace, was a leading agricultural expert of his day. "Uncle Henry," as he was popularly known, has been called one of the great men of Iowa. His family carried on a leadership in national politics into the mid-twentieth century.

Uncle Henry began his life in Iowa as a minister at Davenport, resigning the ministry when his health failed. He began to farm at Winterset and later became a well-known writer on agricultural matters. He went into journalism, finally founding the farming paper *Wallace's Farmer.*

His influence in agriculture was great throughout the nation. He and his best friend, Tama Jim Wilson, and another friend, Seaman Knapp, helped reorganize the State College at Ames and begin its development into one of the great agricultural institutions, Iowa State University.

Uncle Henry Wallace, his son, Henry C. (called Harry), and Harry's son, Henry A. Wallace, all helped establish the family publishing business.

Uncle Henry never became secretary of agriculture, but his son, Henry C., was secretary under Presidents Harding and Coolidge. He died in office in 1924.

Their son, Henry A. Wallace, was one of the earliest leaders in developing hybrid corn. As a practicing farmer, in early youth he constantly experimented with hybrids. The hybrid corn company he founded became one of the most successful in this field.

When President Franklin D. Roosevelt chose him as secretary of agriculture in 1933, Henry A. Wallace began one of the most controversial careers in United States politics.

The farm policies that Wallace brought to the Roosevelt New Deal were both praised and bitterly opposed. They were based on controlling production in order to keep prices up, and the nation has almost completely controlled its farmers' production in one version or another of this program to this day.

In 1940, President Roosevelt personally selected Wallace to be his running mate for vice president and they both were elected. Four years later, however, Wallace was replaced on the ticket by Harry S. Truman. As it turned out, Wallace's failure to retain the vice presidency cost him the presidency of the United States at Roosevelt's death.

Roosevelt named Wallace secretary of commerce in 1945 and he kept the post under Truman until he resigned a year later.

Henry A. Wallace was a candidate for president in the election of 1948 on the Progressive party ticket against Truman. Although he received no electoral votes, his popular vote totaled more than a million.

SO NEAR AND YET SO FAR

Another Iowa man, William B. Allison, narrowly missed a chance at being president of the United States in the nineteenth century.

Allison, of Dubuque, started his public career in Iowa before the Civil War. In the election of 1862 it occurred to him that the soldiers away from home at the front were still eligible to vote. He started the "soldiers' ballot," which we know as the absentee ballot. This soldiers' vote was just enough to win the election for Allison's Republican party, and it gave him the support of most soldiers.

Allison continued to advance politically until his name began to be mentioned as a presidential possibility. The Iowa Republican nominating convention of 1888 ordered its delegates to see to it that Allison got the nomination for president. Twelve hundred Iowa men and women paraded through Chicago booming the Iowa hopeful.

On the third day of the convention, ballots were taken. Chauncey M. Depew of New York was forced to withdraw. He was furious, blaming the Iowa delegation for undermining his support. On the fifth ballot there was an absolute deadlock. No one knew what to do.

Iowa leaders called for a conference with the undecided states. Massachusetts could support either Benjamin Harrison or Allison; New York could support any candidate it pleased. After strong arguments, the whole group promised to support Allison and break the deadlock. The New York delegates said one of their members was not present, but they were sure it would be all right with him.

To the dismay of the Iowa men, that absent New York member was Chauncey Depew, and with a glint of revenge in his eye he refused to support Allison, so New York threw its weight to Harrison and he was nominated. In spite of this defeat, however, Allison continued his public service for Iowa, serving in the United States Senate longer than any other Iowan, from 1872 to his death in 1908.

I DO NOT CHOOSE TO RUN

Unlike others who wanted various nominations, Samuel Kirkwood was so anxious to keep from being nominated for governor of Iowa at the 1875 convention that he refused to attend the convention. In fact, when he heard a group of his friends had gone, he made them leave the convention.

Kirkwood had served for two terms as Iowa's governor during the Civil War and one term in the United States Senate. He wanted to be returned to the Senate, but the Republicans had a strong desire to draft him for governor.

The convention met on June 30, 1875, in Moore's Opera House in Des Moines. The name Kirkwood began to be whispered, but he hadn't come to the convention.

Samuel J. Kirkwood
portrait by
George Yewell

When a group went to look for his close friends to get their support on the nomination, they were nowhere to be found. Kirkwood had sent a special locomotive to get them out of town and away from temptation. The men had been seen sitting in the cab beside the engineer, with the engine whirling down the tracks toward Kirkwood's home in Iowa City, their hair flying in the wind.

The next day Dr. S. M. Ballard, a startling old man six feet six inches (nearly two meters) tall with a white beard to the waist, nominated Kirkwood anyway.

"By whose authority?" everyone shouted.

"By the authority of the great Republican party of the state of Iowa!" Ballard shouted back.

With much cheering the other candidates quickly withdrew, and Kirkwood was nominated by acclamation. The walls rocked with cheers, but then no one dared telegraph Kirkwood the good news.

Finally, a Mr. Finkbine got up his courage and wired: "This gives

you a hold over the party that neither hell nor Harlan could defeat!''
Harlan was Kirkwood's rival for the senatorship.

No answer.

More wires were sent; still there was no answer.

At last in desperation somebody telegraphed: "Why in thunder don't you accept? ANSWER!''

And meekly the reply came: "If I must, say yes for me.''

Samuel Kirkwood was the first man ever to be elected for a third term as governor of Iowa. He served a year and a half of the term and then resigned to become a senator again. His last public office was as secretary of the interior under President Harrison.

No other man in Iowa history has served as governor, senator, and a member of the president's cabinet.

WITH PEN, BRUSH AND MUSIC STAFF

Iowa has had considerable influence in literature, art, and music.

One of Iowa's best-known native authors was Emerson Hough. He gained his greatest fame through his popular novel *The Covered Wagon,* which was made into one of the earliest of the great and spectacular motion pictures.

Margaret Wilson won the Pulitzer Prize for fiction in 1924 by writing about her native Iowa in its pioneer days. She said that her prize-winning book, *The Able McLaughlins,* was a fictionalized account of her family's life in early Traer.

Wilson, who had also been a missionary to India, later married George Douglas Turner, an English criminologist, and wrote a controversial book in England called *The Crime of Punishment.*

Herbert Quick, Hamlin Garland, Ruth Suckow, Phil Stong, James Norman Hall, and MacKinlay Kantor are noted Iowa writers.

One of the most famous humorists of his day, Ellis Parker Butler, was a native of Muscatine. His book *Pigs Is Pigs* is considered one of the classics of American humor.

Iowa artists with widespread reputations include George H. Yewell, Grant Wood, and J.N. "Ding" Darling.

As a young boy in Iowa City, George Yewell's talent for drawing had been recognized, and friends made it possible for him to study in the East. Then his patron, Judge Charles Mason, sent Yewell to study in Paris at the judge's own expense. At thirty-two Yewell had become one of America's foremost painters in Paris. Later he worked in Italy, and his painting *The Interior of St. Mark's, Venice* is a valued treasure in the New York Metropolitan Museum of Art.

From a stay in Egypt came Yewell's two richly colored *Street Scenes in Cairo,* now the property of the Iowa Memorial Union in Iowa City. Nine portraits of Iowans by Yewell, including his famous portrait of Governor Kirkwood, belong to the state.

As a Master of the National Academy, Yewell saw the introduction and passing of many fads in art, but he continued to paint his lustrous works until almost the end of his ninety-two years, even though he was practically blind for the last ten years.

Among the most widely known paintings of modern times is *American Gothic,* by Grant Wood. This work is a portrait of a farm man and woman standing very stiffly and solemnly in front of their home. It is often caricatured in cartoons and is given frequent publicity in many ways.

One man declared that people such as the man and woman pictured in *American Gothic* do not exist, but Wood replied that the models for the painting were his own close relatives.

Wood painted most of his works in Iowa, using its settings as backgrounds. He was one of the most unusual artists of his day and continues to be remembered.

J.N. "Ding" Darling was awarded the Pulitzer Prize for the best cartoon published in 1923. Throughout his long career, Darling was recognized as one of the nation's leading cartoonists.

In the field of music, the most renowned musician associated with the state was not a native. In fact, he resided only a short time in Iowa, but the memory of his stay lingers in the state and in his music. This was the famous Czech composer Antonin Dvorak.

Dvorak had arrived in New York in 1892, but the speed and noise of the city troubled him. He had little time to compose, and when he did he often ended by throwing the unfinished piece out the window.

His assistant, J.J. Kovarik, was a native of Spillville, Iowa, and he told his employer of the little town's peaceful, beautiful setting and its many Czech residents. Dvorak decided to visit Iowa in the spring. So one day in June 1893, Dvorak, his wife and their six children, his assistant, and a maid arrived in that quiet northeast Iowa village. Within three days, Dvorak had sketched his *String Quartet in F Major* and had finished it by the end of twelve days.

Although Dvorak did not write his greatest work, the symphony *From the New World,* in Spillville, the composer made an important change in this work. He added the effective trombone parts to the final movement during his Spillville stay.

He also finished a *String Quintet in E Flat* while in Iowa.

Dvorak was principally interested in picking up native Indian melodies. On a trip to Minnesota, he visited Minnehaha Falls. There he got the inspiration for a new piece, but had no music paper. He is said to have jotted some notes down on his stiff shirt cuff before returning to Iowa.

When he decided to look for the shirt, Dvorak found it had just been sent to the wash. His wife, so the story goes, was lucky enough to rescue the precious notes from going into the suds. From these shirt-cuff notes came his famous *Opus 100, The "Indian Lament."*

Spillville also had its attractions for Dvorak's oldest daughter. She planned to elope in the fall with a local boy. When "Papa" Dvorak heard of this, he became furious and ordered everyone to pack. They left Spillville the very next day.

A popular composer of the mid-twentieth century is a native of Mason City. Meredith Willson's hometown became forever associated with him in the public eye when he wrote the musical comedy *The Music Man,* about a fictitious town modeled after Mason City.

MEN OF SCIENCE

Among Iowa's many men of science, two are particularly interesting and unusual. They are George Washington Carver and Dr. James Van Allen.

In 1888 a young man fled the drought in Kansas. He had lived a difficult and unhappy life, mistreated by most of the people he met, because he was black. In Iowa, for the first time, he found complete acceptance and almost complete lack of persecution.

At about twenty-five years of age, George Washington Carver came to Ames and enrolled in the state college there, under the kindly eye of Tama Jim Wilson, then professor of agriculture and head of the Agriculture Department. Carver worked in the dining hall to help pay his expenses.

Tama Jim was the only one from whom he would accept any favors. The young man spent many weekends at the Wilsons' home and Professor Wilson wrote of him: "He is by all means the ablest student we have here." This was recognition and encouragement of a kind too seldom given a young man of his race in those days.

Six-year-old Henry A. Wallace, at Ames with his family, was very fond of George Washington Carver. He later wrote: "It was he who first introduced me to the mysteries of plant fertilization. . . . His faith aroused my natural interest and kindled an ambition to excel in this field. . . . Later on I . . . spent a good many years breeding corn. Perhaps that was partly because this scientist, who belonged to another race, had deepened my appreciation of plants in a way that I could never forget."

Dr. Carver went on to become one of the world's greatest scientists. It was during his stay and his studies in Iowa that he received the means and the encouragement for his great future.

Another famous Iowa scientist, one of the few modern-day persons to give his name to a part of the heavens, is Dr. James Van Allen of the staff of the University of Iowa, a world-renowned authority on the relationship of radiation and space in physics.

Van Allen designed instruments for detecting radiation in space, and space packages containing these instruments were built under his direction. These were orbited by Jupiter C rockets, and the experiments were very successful. Patterns of radiation in space were discovered. These radiation patterns were then named the Van Allen Belts, giving a unique kind of immortality to an outstanding Iowa scientist.

LADIES FIRST AND A FIRST LADY

An unusual group of prominent women have called Iowa home. Noted stage personality Lillian Russell was born at Clinton in 1861 and made her stage debut there. Hope Glenn of Iowa City was a famous opera singer who performed throughout Europe and the United States and appeared in a command performance before Queen Victoria. Mrs. Mamie Eisenhower, wife of the late president, was born in Boone, Iowa. Carrie Chapman Catt, one of the best-known advocates of women's rights, lived at Charles City.

Another fighter for women's rights caused quite a stir in the mid-1850s when she came to Council Bluffs to make her home. Some of the people there were shocked that Amelia Bloomer had come to their city.

A few years before, Mrs. Bloomer had startled the world when her temperance paper, the *Lily,* came out with a large picture of herself in a new costume for women.

Mrs. Bloomer had decided it was time for women to rebel against the domination of men, especially in the matter of clothing. There was no sense, she reasoned, in women being forced to wear clothes so uncomfortable that they actually deformed some of the wearers. Her new costume was a simple one. "The skirt reaches SCARCELY TO THE KNEES," said one shocked account. "A full pantalet gathered in ruffles over the top of the shoe is all that constitutes the Bloomer costume."

Men called the style brazen; women branded it shameless, but women all over the world began to wear "bloomers." Even the Empress Eugenie wore them.

In spite of much criticism, Mrs. Bloomer's lectures on abstinence and the women's right to vote were so much in demand that her health broke, so she came to Iowa, where she was less well known, to get some rest.

Iowans soon found her to be a sincere and sensible woman. When her health returned she became active in women's rights again and served as president of the Iowa women's suffrage movement. In later years she was never seen to wear her famous costume. Asked why, she said it had served its purpose of focusing male attention on the problems of American women.

Another Iowa woman gained worldwide fame as a result of one night of heroism.

Kate Shelley, who was not quite sixteen years old, lived with her mother, brothers, and sisters in a little house close to the place where the North Western Railroad crossed Honey Creek, not far from Moingona. Her father, a railroad man, had been killed at his work about four years before.

On the night of July 6, 1881, a sudden storm caused the creek to flood rapidly, and the Shelley family heard the crash of an engine as it plunged through the bridge into the water. Their only lantern was broken, but Kate pieced one together with the help of an old miner's lamp.

Rushing out into the storm, Kate saw the engineer and fireman clinging to a tree, surrounded by rushing water. There was no way she could help them. Suddenly she remembered that the fast express train was due in a few minutes.

Kate then hurried off toward town, a mile away, to get help for the wrecked trainmen and to warn the express of the washout. Coming to the old wooden trestle over the Des Moines River, she started across on her hands and knees.

The ties on the trestle were two and three feet apart, with jagged spikes sticking out all over them. The bridge, swaying dangerously, seemed almost ready to collapse. A misstep would have sent her into the swollen river, but she kept on for what seemed like hours. At last, cut and bleeding, she reached the other side and set out for town, arriving just in time to warn the express and send out rescuers for the marooned engineer and fireman.

For days afterward newspaper reporters swarmed over the Shelley farmhouse. Papers from around the world called the Iowa girl a heroine. Kate spent three months in bed recovering from the shock and the excitement.

For her service, the railroad company gave her $100 in cash, a lifetime pass, and a position as station agent in Moingona. The railroad employees presented her a gold watch and chain.

The Iowa legislature donated $200 cash, a gold medal, and gave her the thanks of the state. She received gifts from all parts of the country. People wrote asking for pieces of her dress, slivers from the bridges, or photographs as souvenirs.

At her death in 1912, the railroad company contributed a special train for her funeral party.

Hundreds of poems and stories were written about the event. The new bridge across the Des Moines River where the old trestle had stood was called the Kate Shelley. Visitors to the historical library at Des Moines can still see the little lantern she pieced together from scraps for the emergency.

THE WEST: WILD OR PRETEND?

Noted lawman Wyatt Earp was two when his family moved to Pella, Iowa, where he lived until he was eleven. A romantic television version of his life has made his name a household word.

William Cody was later known by a much more famous name. At age eleven he put on his first Wild West Show in Dennis Barnes's pasture near Le Claire, Iowa. His bucking bronco was an old black mare, and three little boys served as Indians, cowboys, and audience.

When the Cody family moved to Kansas, Bill's father was stabbed because of his feeling against slavery. Bill took over the man's job for the family. At twelve Bill could shoot and ride as well as an adult and had already killed an Indian warrior.

As a young man, Cody learned the Indian language and became a noted scout; finally he hired on as a buffalo hunter for a railroad. Billy Comstock, another buffalo hunter, claimed to be the greatest buffalo killer on the prairies, so a match between the two Bills was arranged.

The one who killed the most buffalo in a given time period would receive $500 and the title of Buffalo Bill. Cody killed sixty-nine and Comstock forty-six; so Cody received the name that stayed with him for the rest of his life.

68

Buffalo Bill's Wild West Show & Rough Riders poster.

Buffalo Bill's friend, author Ned Buntline, popularized him in hundreds of Western stories, and he became the hero of the West.

One day someone asked him to take a part in a play. Cody had never been on the stage before, and he had only four days to learn his part. Consequently, on the opening night he couldn't remember a single line, but made up the part as he went along; he made a great hit and became a popular actor.

Cody decided that the public would be interested in more action on the stage, so he presented his first Wild West Show at Omaha in

1883. During the next three years his show made a grand tour of the country, including Cody's home state of Iowa, and ended up in New York City.

In 1887, Cody toured England and played before Queen Victoria. The show opened with a ferocious Indian fight. Then came a buffalo hunt with Cody doing some fancy shooting. As a grand finale, the whole show was carried away on a terrible Western tornado.

The queen greatly enjoyed the "bucking ponies," and she presented Buffalo Bill with a jeweled crest. He repeated his performance for the kings of Saxony, Denmark, and Greece; the Queen of Belgium; the Crown Prince of Austria; and the Prince of Wales.

Some time after his return to America, however, Cody suffered both financial and health problems. Toward the end of his life, Cody was very sick but needed money so badly that he joined the Sels-Floto Circus. For every performance he was pushed up on his horse; and at the end of his act he fell off exhausted.

William "Buffalo Bill" Cody died a broken and penniless man, but his name still lives as America's great frontier showman.

OTHER OUTSTANDING IOWANS

Adrian "Cap" Anson, whose father founded Marshalltown, Iowa, became one of the greatest figures in nineteenth-century baseball. He is a member of the Baseball Hall of Fame.

Cap Anson may be even more famous, however, for "discovering" another Iowa man. Anson put William Ashley Sunday, of Nevada, Iowa, on his Chicago White Stockings team in 1883, and Sunday became a baseball sensation. Seven years later, however, Sunday quit baseball and became a YMCA worker at one-sixth his former salary.

From there he went into an evangelistic career that made him one of the best-known and best-liked men of his time. He loved dramatic effects in the pulpit. He leaped over the pulpit as easily as he had leaped for a high fly ball. If he became too warm, he would rip off his coat, then his vest, then tie and collar.

He might roll on the floor, tear his hair, or swear in the pulpit, but his sermons had such sincere warmth and such a real message that thousands sought conversion.

With the faithful aid of Ma Sunday and his other helpers, Billy Sunday preached almost to his last day, as someone said, "as if he were at bat in the last inning of a championship game with the bases full and two men out."

Clarence Chamberlain of Denison, Iowa, was one of the famous early aviators. In 1927, shortly after Charles Lindbergh's flight, Chamberlain and Charles Levine flew nonstop from New York to Germany. They had beaten Lindbergh's nonstop distance record, and when the fliers came back to America, towns from New York to Denison honored them.

One of the unique political figures of his time was Harold E. Hughes, governor from 1963 to 1969, and then senator from Iowa, who gave up his political career in 1974 to enter religious service. Before this time he had frequently been mentioned as a Democratic presidential prospect.

Teaching and Learning

For many years Iowa had the highest literacy rate in the nation. It now shares that honor with South Dakota and Nevada. This means that a larger percentage of the residents of the three states can read and write than in the other states of the Union.

Iowa is home to thirty-one colleges and universities and twenty-one community colleges.

The oldest college in the state, with a record of continuous operation, is Iowa Wesleyan College, established as Mount Pleasant Institute in 1842. The school is claimed to be the oldest degree-granting institution west of the Mississippi.

The state legislature provided for a state university in 1847, but not until 1855 was there enough income to offer courses of instruction to students.

These courses covered subjects in nine departments: ancient languages, modern languages, intellectual philosophy, moral philosophy, history, natural history, mathematics, natural philosophy, and chemistry. Because the entire staff consisted of Chancellor Amos Dean and six other professors, there were more departments than teachers.

Certain combinations of study in these departments led to the degree of bachelor of science or bachelor of arts. If a student took work in all nine of the departments, according to the university catalog, he or she was awarded a doctor of philosophy degree.

The entire student body, fifteen men and four women, was on hand at Iowa City in June 1858 to see Edson Smith receive the first collegiate degree ever granted by the University of Iowa.

In 1859 the university practically suspended operations, opening again in 1860. It has been in continuous operation ever since.

A leading department of the university today is the Medical Center, which has been called "one of the nation's outstanding health units."

Opposite: Bell tower at Iowa State University of Science and Technology.

Among the many unique achievements at the Medical Center was the work of Dr. Arthur Steindler in orthopedics; he pioneered many of the present-day practices of bone care, treatment, straightening and grafting, and other orthopedic practices.

Some of the most significant research now being done is in the study of Parkinson's disease.

The American College Testing Program of the university is only one of the many testing programs that has made the institution a leader in all kinds of educational tests. Dr. E.F. Lindquist, director of the testing program, designed unique electronic scoring machines for the tests. Lindquist also originated the famous Iowa Tests of Educational Development, which are almost universally used. Another widely used test series is the Iowa Tests of Basic Skills.

As noted earlier, the university became well known in the field of space research because of the work of Dr. James Van Allen and his colleagues.

Iowa was the first state to accept the provisions of the Morrill Land Grant Act, which was designed to assist colleges in teaching agriculture and mechanic arts.

Iowa State College at Ames (now Iowa State University), established in 1858, became the first of the land-grant colleges in the country, and for a hundred years Iowa has been a leader in land-grant affairs.

Because Iowa is the leading producer of food crops, it was only natural that the most important early work of the college at Ames was in agriculture, and the College of Agriculture is still one of the world leaders. The Agricultural Research Service of the United States Department of Agriculture, near Ames, began operating the National Animal Disease Laboratory in 1961.

Iowa State also began its leadership early in the field of home economics instruction.

The unusual services of Iowa State scientists, and especially of Dr. F.H. Spedding, in World War II led to the creation of the Institute for Atomic Research, which operates the Ames Laboratory of the United States Atomic Energy Commission. A $4,500,000 research reactor was opened at the Ames Laboratory in 1963.

Carver Hall, Iowa State University

Since its beginning in 1876, the University of Northern Iowa at Cedar Falls (formerly Iowa State Teachers College) has been a leader in the training of educators. The university now offers a wide range of educational programs.

In addition to the state institutions, Iowa has many leading private colleges. Grinnell College is frequently listed as one of the country's best liberal arts colleges. Drake University in Des Moines is one of the largest private institutions in Iowa. Among the many outstanding features of Cornell College at Mount Vernon is the traditional annual appearance of the Chicago Symphony Orchestra in May.

Enchantment of Iowa

BEAUTIFUL LAND

Very little is really known about the origin of the word Iowa, except of course that it came through the Ioway Indians. One thought is that it is taken from an Algonquin Indian word meaning "beautiful land."

Although it is a beautiful land, Iowa does not have the reputation of a popular vacation state. Yet millions of people from outside the state visit Iowa every year, even though many are only passing through. Many of them discover the state's unusual variety of attractions, including state parks, state monuments, a national monument, and even several covered bridges.

Visitors to Iowa might well begin their tour at Dubuque, where the state's first major development occurred. One of the most conspicuous reminders of the early days was the old shot tower, where the lead of nearby mines was turned into shot for primitive guns. Dubuque is different from the normally flat Iowa towns. Its high bluffs give it a picturesque quality. The old cable car that runs up and down the bluff has long been a major Dubuque attraction.

Beautiful Eagle Point Park, overlooking the locks and dam of the Mississippi; the oldest log cabin in Iowa; nearby Crystal Lake Cave; and New Melleray Abbey are other Dubuque points of interest.

The *Dubuque Visitor* was begun in May 1836, the first newspaper published in Iowa. It is now the *Telegraph Herald.*

Not far from Dubuque are three state parks of particular interest. Devil's Backbone Park, established in 1920, was the first state park in Iowa. Bixby State Park is known for its ice cave, and White Pine Hollow Forest contains the largest stand of white pine timber in Iowa. Many of the trees are more than two hundred years old.

North of Dubuque on the Mississippi, is McGregor, with its nearby Pike's Peak State Park, where the view of the Mississippi and

Opposite: Fall colors along the trail at Effigy Mounds National Monument.

the mouth of the Wisconsin River on the opposite shore is listed among the notable scenes in the country. Pike's Peak Park is also known for its colored sandstone area, from which Iowa's famous sand pictures originated.

Slightly farther north is the only national monument in Iowa, Effigy Mounds. One of the effigy figures is that of an enormous bear, 137 feet (42 meters) long and 70 feet (21 meters) across the shoulders.

The northeastern corner of Iowa, where only one glacier covered the land, contains the scenic Little Switzerland.

Decorah has been called the "center of Norwegian culture in the United States." The Norwegian-American Historical Museum is located there. Nearby Wonder Cave has a room with a ceiling 150 feet (46 meters) high, located 200 feet (61 meters) underground.

Spillville still preserves the house where the great composer

Folk dancing at the Nordic Fest, Decorah.

Antonin Dvorak lived during his stay there and the church in which he played the organ. A monument at Spillville pays tribute to the composer's Iowa visit.

The Bily Brothers museum at Spillville is the only one of its kind. For many years the Bily Brothers carved and fashioned a very large number of extraordinary clocks. This unique display is on exhibit and in operation for visitors to the museum.

Fort Atkinson is only a short distance away. This fort was the only one of its kind built for its particular purpose. It was not created to protect the settlers but to keep the Winnebago Indians from being harmed by the warlike Sioux. Today, portions of the fort have been restored so that visitors may see a pioneer installation of this type.

To the west is New Hampton, noted for its annual petunia displays. Still farther west, but considered a part of the northeast Iowa region, is Mason City.

Mason City keeps up its tradition as the "home" of Meredith Willson's *Music Man* with its annual North Iowa Band Festival, one of the outstanding events of its kind.

Nearby Clear Lake is one of the state's leading resort areas.

A BROWN CHURCH AND OTHER THINGS COLORFUL

Iowa's most famous church is not a great cathedral but a small wooden building in what was the thriving village of Bradford. In 1857, Dr. William Pitts, a songwriter, visited Bradford. He was much pleased with the beauty of the tiny wooded valley close to the town and remarked what a beautiful setting it would make for a church.

Dr. Pitts returned to his home in Wisconsin and wrote a song about his dream church. When he came back to Bradford in 1864, he was amazed to find a church on the very spot where he had put it in his song. It was even painted brown as was the song's church.

That song was "The Little Brown Church in the Vale," and it soon became quite popular. The famous Fiske Jubilee Singers sang it all across America, and many of the courts of Europe heard of Iowa's Little Brown Church from the same group.

Now the Little Brown Church, near Nashua, is one of the country's most popular wedding sites.

On the Cedar River below Nashua is Waterloo, a leading manufacturing city. The city is the site of the great John Deere tractor plant, often said to be the largest of its kind in the world, and the Rath Packing Company, once considered the largest single meat-packing plant.

A pioneer Waterloo manufacturer, William "Bill" Galloway, is known as one of the most prominent developers of mail-order merchandising. His Galloway Company's national advertising campaign on "splitting the melon" made the phrase famous and was one of the earliest of all such advertising promotions. It made his farm machinery company a leader in its field for many years.

Waterloo is also the home of one of the country's unique and best-known fairs, the Dairy Cattle Congress. This show has long been recognized as the oustanding exhibition of dairy cattle and draft horses.

Not far from Waterloo is Traer, the home of Tama Jim Wilson. His sister, Jean Wilson, of Traer, was a pioneer in teaching the blind. When she was a young woman, the blind were considered useless and were put away in asylums. One of these asylums was at Vinton. Jean Wilson joined the staff at Vinton with the determination that the blind could be taught. She transported an entire class of pupils to Des Moines and demonstrated their learning skills before the legislature. The legislators were so impressed that they appropriated the money for a school for the blind at Vinton. The Braille and sight-saving school there is still one of the leaders in its field.

In a unique gesture of appreciation for her services, the state "gave" Miss Wilson her wedding, when she married S.P. Smith.

At Tama is found Iowa's only Indian reservation. Visitors may see the annual powwow of the Mesquakie and buy their craft products. They are skillful in weaving, basket making, bead work, and leather. They maintain their wickiups (resembling tepees), but only for special visits and ceremonies.

Directly to the east is Cedar Rapids, with the greatest volume of manufacture in the state. The Masonic Library there claims the most

The Cedar Rapids city government buildings and Linn County Courthouse are located on an island in the Cedar River.

complete Masonic collection in the United States. To the north of Cedar Rapids is Stone City, where Grant Wood headed a famous art colony. Interest in art grew and after Wood's death, the Anamosa Paint 'n Palette Club was organized. The club purchased the Antioch School as a memorial to Wood.

South of Cedar Rapids is a group of communities with one of the most famous names in Iowa—Amana.

On a peaceful hillside on the Iowa River in the summer of 1855 a plain but sturdily built village was rapidly taking shape. The energetic leader in this enterprise was well equipped for building work, as he had been a carpenter in Germany.

That man was Christian Metz, and he had called his followers from New York State to settle on the 26,000 acres (10,522 hectares) of rich Iowa soil and heavily wooded uplands that had just been purchased for their use.

81

These people, who had emigrated from Germany not many years before, called their new little village Amana, because its site resembled that of a village that Solomon had called Amana, and the word itself meant "remain true."

This simple-living but gifted folk remained true to the principle that bound them together. Their faith that everything they did was inspired by a benevolent God never faltered, and they prospered.

They shared all property. Everyone worked up to the limit of his ability, but no one worked beyond his strength.

Women with children under two years of age did no community work at all. Aged people received almost lavish attention. Each person had his own bedroom and sitting room to furnish as he or she wished, which gave them a feeling of personal ownership. Everyone was made to feel that he was a happy and necessary part of society.

Amana-blue calicos and woolens were soon sold throughout the country and, keeping pace with every advance in farming methods, Amana residents raised bountiful crops that brought top prices. In 1920 the total value of their real and personal property was listed at $2,102,984. Amana's mills and factories, paintless houses and spotless kitchens, and enormous fresh vegetable and bright flower gardens have dotted the Iowa countryside, as a constant reminder of one of the few successful enterprises in community living.

Today, however, the community ownership has been changed to stock interest, and the earlier forms of sharing have been given up, but the enterprise continues to prosper. Much of interest concerning the older days remains to the visitor in the seven Amana villages.

The principal fame of Amana now comes from its world renowned leadership in the manufacture of refrigerators, freezers, and other products.

Not far from the Amanas is Iowa City, home of the University of Iowa. One of the unusual attractions at the university is its renowned bagpipe band, one of the largest and most colorful in the world. It has traveled widely to carry the university name across the United States and abroad.

Iowa's most widely heralded building, the Old Stone Capitol, is located at Iowa City, where it is used as the university's administration building. In use since 1842, it is said to be the "most beautiful building in the state."

East of Iowa City is the quiet and peaceful village of West Branch, where Herbert Hoover was born. Here the visitor may see the touching statue contributed by the children of Belgium, who gave their pennies as a tribute to the man who kept their country from starvation during World War I. In addition to the birthplace home and burial site and the Hoover Library, there is also a replica of the blacksmith shop where Herbert's father was the smithy.

To the north and east is Maquoketa Caves State Park. Here, as a surprise to most visitors, is a natural bridge with a span fifty feet (fifteen meters) high and a balanced rock weighing seventeen tons (fifteen metric tons). The caves were the home of prehistoric people, whose relics have been found there.

To the south is Davenport, the largest Iowa city on the Mississippi. This was the home of Colonel B.J. Palmer, the father of chiropractic treatment. The Palmer School at Davenport once trained a large percentage of the country's chiropractors. The Palmer Museum is a Davenport attraction. Colonel Palmer was also a pioneer owner of Iowa radio stations and was widely known for his colorful personality.

Somewhat farther south, Muscatine is home of freshwater pearl buttons and delicious melons. It claims to be the only city in the world bearing that name.

Another Iowa river town, Burlington, was capitol of Wisconsin Territory in 1837 and capital of Iowa Territory in 1838. Snake Alley in Burlington is claimed by some to be the "crookedest street in the world." Burlington's first newspaper, the *Hawk-Eye Gazette,* is sometimes said to have given the state its nickname of the Hawkeye State, although there are several other stories about the origin of the name.

South of Burlington is Fort Madison. The state penitentiary located here is the oldest penal institution west of the Mississippi. Crossing the Mississippi at Fort Madison is the largest railroad bridge of its kind in the world. Fort Madison hosts the annual Tri-State Championship Rodeo, generally ranked as one of the ten best in the world. The Sheaffer Pen Company, where the founder, W.A. Sheaffer, developed the fountain pen, is also headquartered here.

Keokuk, at the far southeastern tip of the state, gives its name to the mighty dam across the Mississippi. Here is the grave of Chief Keokuk, who in turn gave his name to the city.

Type for the first city directory of Keokuk was mostly hand set in his brother's Keokuk print shop by Samuel Clemens, who became the famous author Mark Twain.

Lee County is the location of the first schoolhouse in Iowa, which has been reproduced as a memorial. Also in Lee County is Civil War Memorial Park near Croton, location of the only Civil War activity in Iowa.

In nearby Lacey-Keosauqua Park is Ely's Ford, where the Mormons crossed the Des Moines River. After being driven out of Illinois, the Mormons started migrating across Iowa in large numbers, beginning in February 1846. They established eight camps or stations across southern Iowa on their route to the Far West. Many of these stations became the basis for permanent settlements. By the middle of May, sixteen thousand Mormons had crossed Iowa.

Some of the Mormons broke away from the main group and established the Reorganized Church of Jesus Christ of Latter Day Saints. This group had its headquarters in Lamoni, Iowa, until 1907.

At Keosauqua, the courthouse is said to be the oldest west of the Mississippi still in use.

To the northwest, Pella was founded by seven hundred Dutch people who came to Iowa for religious freedom under their preacher-leader Dominie Scholte. They were a wealthy group and the community prospered. Today, the tulips of Pella at the annual tulip time provide one of the country's leading blossom festivals.

North of Pella lies Grinnell. Josiah Bushnell Grinnell was a Congregational minister when he visited the noted publisher Horace Greeley to ask advice about his future career. Greeley is supposed to have said, "Go west, young man; go west and grow up with the country." This phrase, "Go west, young man," has become one of the best known in our history.

Grinnell took Greeley's advice and went to Iowa in 1854. He

founded the town now bearing his name, which was then not much more than open prairie. Lots were reserved for a college campus. The college opened a year later. Other lots were sold with an agreement that the lots would be forfeited back to Grinnell or his estate if liquor were ever sold on them.

Grinnell's house was a station on the Underground Railroad and many slaves were helped in their escape.

To the west is Newton, where a one-time farm boy became the Washing Machine King. F.L. Maytag began in 1909 to manufacture a washing machine operated by hand. It had been designed by Howard Snyder. Two years later the men attached a motor to their machine, thus introducing the motorized washing machine.

In 1922, Snyder perfected a square aluminum tub, and the Maytag Company took over a leading position in the industry. In 1948 the company brought the first automatic washer to the public.

NEVER ANY MONKS

There is a widespread belief that the name Des Moines means "of the monks." This is the translation of the similar French term. But there never were any monks in the region, and most authorities now feel that the word comes from the Indian words *moin* or *moingona*. These words were altered by the French and other early visitors to Iowa until they reached their present form.

The name Des Moines had been applied to the river on early maps, and when a fort was set up at the fork of the Des Moines and Raccoon rivers in 1843, it was called Fort Des Moines. A settlement grew up around the fort and in 1851 the city of Fort Des Moines was incorporated. Later, the name became Des Moines. The capital was moved there in 1857.

The 22-carat gold dome of the state capitol building, looming on its hilltop, can be seen for many miles around Des Moines. The building was begun in 1871 and dedicated thirteen years later. Much of the granite used in its construction was cut from glacial boulders found on the Iowa prairies.

The state capitol building in Des Moines.

Iowa's capitol is noted for its interior decoration. The mural *Westward* by Edwin H. Blashfield is one of the best known in the country. It represents the coming to Iowa of the various pioneer groups.

Battle flags carried by Iowa regiments in the Civil War and later wars are preserved in the capitol as prized mementos of the sacrifices of Iowa men and women in war.

The ninety-three-acre (thirty-eight-hectare) grounds of the Iowa capitol have been called the "largest and most beautiful setting for a state capitol." Willson Alexander Scott settled on what is now the capitol grounds, and he donated ten acres (four hectares) of this land as the site for a capitol building. Scott is buried on the capitol grounds, where a granite memorial marks the location.

Other memorials in Capitol Park include those to William B. Allison and Christopher Columbus, and the Soldiers' and Sailors' Monument, built in 1889 at a cost of $150,000.

There are numerous state-owned buildings in Des Moines, including state office buildings and the State Historical Building.

The historical museum has many fine exhibits. One of the most noted of these is a set of four slabs of fossil crinoids, including a particularly rare slab showing the remains of starfish. Altogether, 183 rare fossils are seen in the slabs; this is considered the finest collection of its kind in existence. The museum is outstanding in the world in this type of material.

The Des Moines Civic Center includes City Hall, Municipal Court Building, Public Library, Post Office, U.S. Court House, and the YMCA.

An art museum, said to be unique in museum design, and a large veterans' memorial auditorium are other Des Moines points of interest.

The annual state fair at Des Moines is one of the largest and best known fairs anywhere. It was the setting for Phil Stong's famous book *State Fair,* which was made into two well-known motion pictures.

Because of its large insurance business, Des Moines is known as The Hartford of the West. Many insurance companies have their home offices in Des Moines.

Another leading Des Moines activity is publishing. Many large publishing companies originated in Des Moines and retain their headquarters there.

Among Des Moines' principal publishers is the Cowles organization, which published *Look Magazine* and leading newspapers in Minnesota, as well as the *Des Moines Register* and *Tribune.*

Another of the country's leading producers of magazines and books, the Meredith Publishing Company, has its principal operation in Des Moines. Meredith publishes *Better Homes and Gardens, Apartment Life,* and *Successful Farming* magazines, in addition to books.

Des Moines is particularly known as a center for farm journal publishing. In addition to *Successful Farming, Wallace's Farmer* is another popular farm publication.

Drake University at Des Moines has continued to expand its campus, with several major buildings of prize-winning modern design. Among other distinctions, the university is well-known throughout the world for its annual Drake Relays, one of the country's oldest and most noteworthy track and field events.

Near Des Moines is a notable farm museum, re-creating typical farms of several periods.

North of Des Moines, the campus of Iowa State University, at

Ames, has been generally recognized as one of the most beautiful anywhere.

In nearby Marshall County is the unique Fisher Community Center, exhibiting art by Utrillo, Cassatt, and other prominent artists.

Near Boone are Ledges State Park and Pilot Knob, which served as a guide for early travelers.

WESTERN IOWA

A majority of Iowa's remaining covered bridges are found in Madison County, near Winterset.

Guthrie County is the location of one of the country's unique preserves. When the pioneers came to Iowa, they found the wonderful prairies of enormously tall grasses which had remained unchanged for countless years. Almost all of the original prairie has been plowed or "civilized" in some other manner.

The forty-acre (sixteen-hectare) Virgin Prairie Area preserve in Guthrie County is one of the few remaining locations where Iowa prairie can be seen as it looked in the time of the first European settlement.

In far southwestern Iowa, Tabor is the site of John Brown's former headquarters.

At Council Bluffs, two memorials remind visitors of history. The Lincoln Monument recalls the visit of the great man to Council Bluffs, and the Golden Spike Monument commemorates the completion of the transcontinental railroad, with its eastern terminal at Council Bluffs. A golden spike was driven into the track in Utah where the east and west sections of the railroad met. The Council Bluffs monument to this event has the shape of an enormous railroad spike.

Rainbow Drive at Council Bluffs is one of the most scenic roads in the state.

Northeast of Council Bluffs, in the Woodbine area, are Indian mounds covering a four-block area.

Sioux City is the third largest livestock and grain center in the United States. With its symphony orchestra, civic ballet, theatres, and arts center, it has been called the Cultural Mecca of the Plains.

At Sioux City is the grave of War Eagle. The first settler, a French trapper from Canada, married War Eagle's daughter. The famous old chief took a kindly attitude toward the settlers, and the Sioux City region developed rapidly.

The memorial to Sergeant Floyd of the Lewis and Clark party, on the bluffs overlooking the Missouri where his fellow explorers laid him to rest, is an especially fine and much visited monument.

At Pocahantas is a statue to the famous Indian maiden, whose name was taken by the town.

To the north is the popular recreational area centered on Spirit Lake and the Okiboji Lakes. Near Spirit Lake, visitors may see the restored cabin where the Gardner family was murdered by Indians and from which young Abigail Gardner was kidnapped. The book *Spirit Lake* by MacKinlay Kantor is based on this time of trouble. Actually, the scene of the massacre took place at West Okiboji Lake, not Spirit Lake.

In far northwest Iowa are two spots of particular interest. Ocheyedan Mound is the highest point in Iowa. It was built up 170 feet (52 meters) above the surrounding area by prehistoric people thousands of years before Europeans came into the country. Near Larchwood at Gitchie Manitou State Park is an area where sturdy quartzite rocks can be seen. These are believed to be an incredible 500 million years old.

The people who have lived on the land between the two great rivers have fought, struggled, labored, laughed, and grown in wealth and culture through the years. As it was in the past, so it also is now. This year, next year, and every year that people live in the state, new and important people of various nationalities will be writing themselves into the pages of Iowa history.

Handy Reference Section

Instant Facts

Became the 29th state, December 18, 1846
Capital—Des Moines, settlement beginning in 1843
Nickname—The Hawkeye State
State motto—"Our liberties we prize and our rights we will maintain"
State bird—Eastern Goldfinch
State flower—Wild Rose
State tree—Oak
State stone—Geode
State song—"The Song of Iowa," by S.H.M. Byers
Area—55,941 square miles (144,887 square kilometers)
Rank in area—23rd
Greatest length (north to south)—209 miles (336 kilometers)
Greatest width (east to west)—301 miles (484 kilometers)
Geographic center—Story, 5 miles (8 kilometers) northeast of Ames
Highest point—1,670 feet (509 meters), Ocheyedan Mound, Osceola County
Lowest point—447 feet (136 meters)
Mean elevation—1,100 feet (335 meters)
Number of counties—99
Population—2,908,000 (1980 projection)
Rank in population—25th
Population density—51.9 per square mile (20 per square kilometer), 1980 projection
Rank in density—29th
Population center—In Marshall County, 10 miles (16 kilometers) southwest of Marshalltown
Illiteracy—0.5%
Birthrate—13.4 per 1,000
Infant mortality rate—15.5 per 1,000 births
Physicians per 100,000—103

Principal cities—		
Des Moines	201,404	(1970 census)
Cedar Rapids	110,642	
Davenport	98,469	
Sioux City	85,925	
Waterloo	75,533	

You Have a Date with History

1673—Marquette and Jolliet see Iowa
1762—Spain takes Louisiana Territory, including Iowa
1796—Land grant in Iowa to Julien Dubuque

1803 — United States buys Louisiana Territory
1804 — Lewis and Clark expedition
1808 — Fort Madison military post established
1833 — First legal settlement permitted
1838 — Iowa becomes a separate territory
1846 — Statehood
1854 — First railroad
1857 — Des Moines made state capital
1867 — North Western Railroad is first to span state
1869 — Transcontinental railroad finished
1877 — Iowa takes leadership in hog production
1913 — Dam at Keokuk completed
1914 — First air-mail flight
1952 — First billion-dollar corn crop
1961 — National Animal Disease Laboratory opened at Ames
1963 — Institute for Atomic Research opens $4,500,000 reactor at Ames
1973 — State's first nuclear power plant completed in Palo
1976 — Democrats win control of legislature
1979 — Robert Ray begins tenth year as governor

The Governors of Iowa

Ansel Briggs 1846-1850
Stephen P. Hempstead 1850-1854
James W. Grimes 1854-1858
Ralph P. Lowe 1858-1860
Samuel J. Kirkwood 1860-1864
William M. Stone 1864-1868
Samuel Merrill 1868-1872
Cyrus C. Carpenter 1872-1876
Samuel J. Kirkwood 1876-1877
Joshua G. Newbold 1877-1878
John H. Gear 1878-1882
Buren R. Sherman 1882-1886
William Larrabee 1886-1890
Horace Boies 1890-1894
Frank D. Jackson 1894-1896
Francis M. Drake 1896-1898
Leslie M. Shaw 1898-1902
Albert B. Cummins 1902-1908
Warren Garst 1908-1909

Beryl F. Carroll 1909-1913
George W. Clarke 1913-1917
William L. Harding 1917-1921
N.E. Kendall 1921-1925
John Hammill 1925-1931
Daniel W. Turner 1931-1933
Clyde L. Herring 1933-1937
Nelson G. Kraschel 1937-1939
George A. Wilson 1939-1943
Bourke B. Hickenlooper 1943-1945
Robert D. Blue 1945-1949
William S. Beardsley 1949-1954
Leo Elthon 1954-1955
Leo A. Hoegh 1955-1957
Herschel C. Loveless 1957-1961
Norman A. Erbe 1961-1963
Harold E. Hughes 1963-1969
Robert D. Ray 1969-

Index

95

PICTURE CREDITS

ABOUT THE AUTHOR

With the publication of his first book for school use when he was twenty, **Allan Carpenter** began a career as an author that has spanned more than 135 books. After teaching in the public schools of Des Moines, Mr. Carpenter began his career as an educational publisher at the age of twenty-one when he founded the magazine *Teachers Digest.* In the field of educational periodicals, he was responsible for many innovations. During his many years in publishing, he has perfected a highly organized approach to handling large volumes of factual material: after extensive traveling and having collected all possible materials, he systematically reviews and organizes everything. From his apartment high in Chicago's John Hancock Building, Allan recalls, "My collection and assimilation of materials on the states and countries began before the publication of my first book." Allan is the founder of Carpenter Publishing House and of Infordata International, Inc., publishers of *Issues in Education* and *Index to U. S. Government Periodicals.* When he is not writing or traveling, his principal avocation is music. He has been the principal bassist of many symphonies, and he managed the country's leading non-professional symphony for twenty-five years.

96